Effective

Presentations

How to Present
Facts, Figures, and
Ideas Successfully

Effective

Presentations

How to Present Facts, Figures, and Ideas Successfully

Edward Hodnett

Parker Publishing Company, Inc.

West Nyack, N. Y.

PRINTED IN THE UNITED STATES OF AMERICA
B&P

Acknowledgments

The present book is a complete rewriting of a manual prepared a few years ago for the guidance of executives, chemists, engineers, salesmen, and other professional employees of Dow Corning Corporation. I thank the officers of Dow Corning for permission to use that manuscript as a working draft, and my colleagues for suggestions on ways to expand it.

Contents

II

GRAPHICS AND OTHER AUDIO-VISUAL AIDS

III

MAKING ORAL PRESENTATIONS

Effective

Presentations

How to Present
Facts, Figures, and
Ideas Successfully

1

The Importance of

Presentations

The word "presentation" is an example of how the English language flexes to the shape of new meanings. None of the dictionary definitions quite covers the specialized sense in which the word has come to be widely used in business, industry, government, and other professions.

A Presentation Is a Specialized Form of Communication

A presentation is first of all a talk that contains expository material, is often persuasive, and frequently involves graphics or other audio-visual aids. The use of audio-visual aids is usually the most distinguishing characteristic of a presentation, but the term is commonly used when no aids are present.

A presentation has the serious purpose of acquainting an audience with information about a specific matter, often with the intent of aiding or influencing decision-making. A talk to a service club about why school millage should be increased is a presentation; one about the outlook for a football team is not. A clergyman submitting his plans for a new Sunday school is making a presentation; delivering a sermon, he is not. The term is loosely used for many talks not considered to be presentations in this book—sermons, for instance. The distinctions are unimportant. The point is that the use of the term presentation for a specialized form of discourse has general sanction.

It is also common to hear the term presentation applied to proposals where sheets of paper are all that is tangible—for instance, when written matter supports a face-to-face request to a foundation for a grant of aid, a bid to a board of education to handle the cafeteria service, or a talk to a technical society about a new molding compound. By extension, such a written statement standing alone is commonly called a presentation.

Normally, then, the two distinguishing features of a presentation are the presence of graphics, written material, or other audiovisual aids and the pervasive effort to secure a predetermined, practical response from the audience.

You are free to dismiss the word as jargon, but salesmen, consultants, advertising men, engineers, architects, government officials, teachers, lawyers, doctors, clergymen, and other people in all walks of life make millions of presentations every day. To them the term is meaningful in designating the specialized nature of this kind of communication.

Good Presentations Are the Mark of a True Professional

As your professional career progresses, the more presentations (both oral and written) you will give, and the more the presentations of the people who work for you will influence your success.

You give oral presentations inside your organization, such as those of a market research director to his top management, a sales manager to his salesmen, or a surgeon to his internes. Much of your success professionally depends on the effectiveness of the presentations you make at group problem-solving sessions within your organization.

Outside oral presentations are given at professional society meetings, at customers' plants, and before civic bodies.

You give formal presentations in conference rooms, classrooms, and auditoriums, and you give informal ones over the telephone, in colleagues' offices, and across luncheon tables.

You give written presentations, as already noted, on the many occasions when written statements accompany oral presentations, as is habitual at professional society meetings, and by extension in all those memoranda, reports, letters, papers, and articles that meet the conditions of our definition of a presentation.

Your professional activities put a premium on your oral and written presentations. This is one of the bench marks of all true professions. If you are an accountant, an advertising supervisor, a physicist, an engineer, or a member of any other business or industrial group, the obligation to communicate in this special way is one chief characteristic that you have in common with members of the legal, medical, teaching, or other professions. In a true profession, as distinct from a trade, what you know and what you can do have to be implemented by your ability to communicate by means of effective oral and written presentations.

A professional, incidentally, is a person who knows exactly what he is doing and does it better than the journeyman performer. When someone says, "Gordie Howe is a real pro!" he does not mean that the great Red Wing plays hockey for money. True, the fellow who plays for pay or works at a craft for pay is more often a pro in this complimentary sense, than the fellow who does so for fun. The person who paints portraits for a living knows things about preparing the surface of his canvas, placing his subject, mixing his colors, choosing his brushes, and a dozen other crucial matters that the talented amateur rarely bothers to learn.

So with the person who makes professional presentations, though he may never be paid directly for them. He has studied the technique of giving presentations so assiduously that he knows *in advance* all the steps he has to take to ensure excellence. Even while he is in the middle of a presentation, he is aware of how well he is doing and what he needs to do to improve the response.

Successful Presentations Are an
Avenue of Advancement

What we are calling a presentation often occurs at times of crucial importance to an enterprise. Therefore, if you make one excellent presentation—just one—it may lead to a significant departmental decision, increase your company's business, help you win a promotion, or elevate you to professional or public leadership. No one has ever been seriously handicapped professionally by lack of skill in after-dinner speaking or essay writing, but many careers have been compromised by poor presentations and many causes lost. The exceptional importance invested in presentations is the justification of this book.

Skill in presentations is just as practical a part of your job and your civic activities as any other. What you know and what you can do are not enough. A corporation president who goes before his board of directors to ask for authorization to build a $10,000,-000 plant cannot get by on his ability to run plants or sell goods. The $10,000,000 decision, with all of the consequences whichever way it goes, rests to a critical degree on how shrewdly he plans his presentation and how well he gives it.

The brilliant scientist, the winning attorney, the influential scholar, the popular public official are almost invariably masters of the presentation. Their success should prove how vital it is to your career that your presentations—in the broad sense of this book—be a totality of planning, practice, and habit.

A certain share of the presentations you give will be competitive. In most instances the competition is covert—you are simply on the program with several others. Yet as speaker succeeds speaker, the audience inevitably compares your presentation with the others. If you bumble, drone, or talk too long, you get low marks. If you are well organized, animated, and economical of time, you get good marks. Since the marks at most meetings run from B to D (with most around C), you have a splendid chance to cover yourself with glory by earning an A.

The impression you make on an audience is to a considerable extent passed on to the organization you represent. If you and your colleagues take the trouble to make your presentations all that they should be, after a while the word will get round: You can always count on those Jones & Smith fellows to give a first-rate presentation; they must be a grade-A firm.

Here is the case history of a presentation essentially as it happened. Petrox, a large petrochemical corporation, is reviewing its business at a luncheon it is giving at its New York headquarters for fifty members of the National Society of Security Analysts. The treasurer of Petrox asks John Ashwood to do a special presentation about the new biochemical division that Ashwood heads. He will have precisely 30 minutes, including a question period.

Ashwood calls in his controller, director of planning, and his director of public relations to help him plan his presentation. The audience is self-defining. These are the men and women who advise banks, mutual funds, insurance companies, and other large investors about the financial health and outlook of companies in which they have invested or may consider investing. In order to arrive at their judgments, analysts study individual company annual reports and other financial records, the economic environment of each company, and its competition. They are especially interested in the way a company is run and its potential for growth.

The situation analysis by Ashwood and his associates is a sobering one. The judgments made by these fifty security analysts can have a significant effect on how Petrox fares on the stock market and whether or not large investors hold, buy, or sell Petrox stock, and at what rate of interest Petrox can borrow millions of dollars for new enterprises. These actions affect the profitability of the company and the welfare of all employees. This background influences the planning of the presentation by Ashwood and his associates.

A secondary element in the situation is a personal one. The success of Ashwood's presentation will be measured not only by the reactions of the security analysts, but also by the treasurer's opinion of how well it enhances the standing of Petrox. Also at the meeting there will be other influential officers of Petrox and members of its board of directors. Ashwood's future is in the hands of these men.

Out of these considerations comes the chief message—the biochemical division of Petrox has had an excellent record of growth and profitability and has even brighter prospects for the future.

Ashwood spends hours writing notes, talking with associates, having slides made up, collecting sample products, and soliloquizing. Alas, the first rehearsal runs an hour and ten minutes. Ashwood burns up time on organization charts, slides of division plants, and, perhaps because of his training as a biochemist, explanations of the structure and characteristics of products.

But Ashwood is an honest, dogged worker. He has plenty of lead time, and he makes note of the suggestions from his staff. He holds three rehearsals with his staff, and he rehearses dozens of times by himself. When he gets up after the luncheon in New York, he is master of his material, and he knows it. He knows that the main elements are now rightly proportioned and exactly what emphasis to give the details.

He disposes of the basic facts about the division in three minutes with the aid of one slide. He emphasizes the high proportion of research and development. He discusses the five product lines by merely holding up a sample of each. Pie-chart slides indicate the large dollar share of the pharmaceutical market held by the biochemical division of Petrox. He reveals plans for entering new markets with new products. Then he gives the final ten minutes to an analysis of sales, reinvestment, and earnings with a projection of doubled growth within five years.

After the guests are gone, the treasurer says, "You did a great job, John." And he almost smiles. For weeks, stories come out in financial papers and business magazines, complimentary references to Petrox pop up, and appreciative letters from the analysts flow back.

Every Executive Is a Director of Presentations

The *you* in these pages is a person who makes presentations. In the broad sense of the word, you are an executive. But as your professional career advances, you will be increasingly responsible for presentations that others make. The degree of your involvement will vary. You may merely decide that a presentation should be made, or you may plan its general attack. You may work out all the details, or you may check the detailed plans of others. You may spend hours coaching someone who is giving a presentation, or you may be a final critic.

However it may be in a specific instance, you will fill all of these roles many times during your professional career. Even the youngest executive finds, with dismay, that his professional success is to a disconcerting degree in the hands of those persons who make presentations under his direction. Beyond your own self interest, you have a responsibility to help all professional persons working for you to become expert in making presentations; to do that, you must first master the subject yourself.

The title "director of presentations" does not exist, but every large organization should have someone with this responsibility. Few do. When the responsibility is recognized at all, it is usually spread among several persons, none of whom has the breadth of experience necessary to direct all phases of presentation-making. An organization considers itself progressive if it has an audio-visual aids department, but such aids are only one relatively mechanical aspect of the job of our hypothetical director of presentations.

In fact, every executive is a director of presentations. Sooner or later you will be one. First, you should have a broad general education, with more than the ordinary understanding of the processes of reasoning.

Second, you should be thoroughly acquainted with the goals, procedures, and policies of your organization. You should always be able to follow the reasoning in the light of the interests of the organization. You do not have to be familiar with all of the material covered in every presentation. However, it certainly helps if you are directing a financial talk to know what key terms such as standard costs, variables, and gross margins mean.

Third, you should be skilled in the organization and expression of thought.

Fourth, you should be knowledgeable in speech techniques.

Fifth, you should have a working acquaintance with graphics, audio systems, projection, and other presentation aids.

A person who acts in the capacity of a director of presentations is unlikely to be strong in all five of the areas noted. If, however, he starts with a broad general education and a conscious awareness of logical methods of reasoning, he can become adept in all the other areas. This process is not reversible.

To be an effective director of presentations, you should enjoy the confidence of the top management of your organization, or at least of that sector in which you function. A person guiding the presentations of a sales force or of a government agency cannot make critical judgments about the material being presented by a member of the organization, unless he can place it within the context of executive thinking.

You cannot direct presentations at the level of technique alone. Not only must you be able to analyze the strengths and weaknesses of a finished presentation; you must, if need be, plan the strategy, sketch the pattern of thought, develop the supporting evidence, and decide what aids should be used. You do not customarily do all this, but you should be able to do it. And you should have the tact and the acceptance from your colleagues to have your suggestions prevail most of the time.

Making a presentation is often a serious occasion—sometimes it is a traumatic one. As a director of presentations, you have to act somewhat in the role of a doctor. For your patient's sake, you must insist on early confrontation with the job in hand, revisions of first plans, rehearsals, changes, and more changes. Inexperienced persons, predictably, react negatively to this pressure. They think such perfectionism absurd; they may even grow hostile, thinking they are being pushed around.

If you are a good director, you will usually learn of such negative reactions when someone comes to thank you for help in what turned out to be a successful presentation. Happily, persons experienced in making presentations—the pros—are perfectionists themselves and welcome critical help without having their vanity hurt. They know that an excellent final presentation comes from gradual improvement of specific parts.

Skilful directors of presentations are as rare as Kirtland's warbler. But they will become more common, because they are badly needed. Meanwhile, as you take a hand in guiding the presentations of your associates, you have an obligation to become more professional in your guidance. You would not take on the job of directing an amateur production of "Gammer Gurton's Needle" without some knowledge of the theater and the business of play directing. You should take much more pains to be prepared to direct a presentation on which a great deal depends, than to direct a play on which nothing much depends.

In directing presentations, you should never forget that your main goal is to make each of the persons you work with self-sufficient. You are a teacher. Every preparatory session is a tutorial. Every presentation is a stepping-stone to better presentations. You are successful when your charges can do without you, or, at least, can do without you if they have to. You fulfill your role best when the persons you have helped become competent to direct others.

Mastery of Presentations Is Part of Your Professional Growth

This book of professional techniques deals with specifics, with what are the least difficult parts of making presentations. In the broader sense your effectiveness depends upon what kind of person you are, how much you know about your subject, and how well educated you are in general.

No matter how well delivered, the presentation of a consultant's recommendation based on unsound evidence or mistaken cause and effect, poor analogy, or any other logical fallacy is unsatisfactory. A technical report that has a serious mathematical error in it is unsatisfactory. A letter to a correspondent that overlooks one of his key questions is unsatisfactory. An otherwise good oral presentation marred by slovenly speech or appearance is unsatisfactory.

Effective Presentations is meant to be a practical guide to specific matters that habitually concern people in industry, business, public affairs, science, and the other professions. The suggestions are precise because the successful execution of any action, from a forward pass in football to sending a spacecraft to photograph a planet, depends on the exact management of many details.

Nothing suggested in this book is meant to be absolute. Some latitude is assumed—is indeed inherent in the philosophy of communication as adjustment to specific circumstances. Nevertheless, these procedures and techniques have been tested on the firing line of actual practice and following them should save time and improve professional performance. In the recommended readings and in your public library you will find more detailed statements about many of the matters discussed here.

If you have a special individual difficulty, do not coddle it. Do something about it. Study regularly by yourself. Take a night course. Join a community group such as the Toastmasters. Above all, ask for criticism and use it. The essence of professional growth is to take positive steps to develop yourself in all respects. You have ample opportunities to improve your presentations; make the most of them.

Your own personal growth is involved. You want to meet the requirements of your job, and you want to meet the highest standards of your profession. But beyond that you want to be as effective a person as you believe you can be. Your own standards for yourself, the highest standards of your profession, your responsibility as an educated citizen, and your own self-directed efforts to keep growing professionally make it imperative for you to give serious attention to both oral and written presentations at all times.

Any well-run organization can set up a systematic procedure for handling presentations. First, all executives should be made aware of the importance of presentations and of their responsibility for all of those made by persons under their direction. All persons who normally make presentations should be given instruction in the various matters covered in this book. Competent help in planning presentations should be available. So should an adequate audio-visual aids department. No one should ever be allowed to make an official presentation without rehearsal and clearance. But in the end, the responsibility lies with you, the individual, to realize how important your presentations are to your organization and to your career and to lift them to the professional level.

Part I
Preparing the
Presentation

2

Planning Your

Strategy

The reaction of the listener or reader tells the difference between a professional presentation and an unskilled one. How clear and easy it all seems, he thinks about the professional presentation; he may even have a sneaking feeling of superiority. He is beguiled into believing that he already knows the same facts and ideas and has arrived at the same conclusions. The unskilled presentation is sometimes difficult, even painful, to follow. It gives rise to questions instead of agreement, to doubts about the competence of the speaker or author, and possibly to antagonism.

The essential difference between a satisfactory presentation and an unsatisfactory one consists almost entirely in what takes place before a speaker gets up to speak or before the reader sees the final draft of a written presentation. A great deal of this difference is attributable to depth of experience. The leaders in any field are usually superior communicators because they understand their subject more thoroughly than others do. Their experience includes not only years of concentrated thinking, but also years of clarification of their thoughts by writing and talking.

Mastering your subject is the most important part of getting ready to make a presentation. Unless you have isolated the main issues, gathered all the relevant data, sorted out the key ideas, and done as much as you are expected to do to solve the problems involved, you are not ready. But even this is not always enough. The secret of presentations of professional competence is the completeness of the preparation. Knowledge of the subject and past experience are part of the preparation, but they are not sufficient to guarantee a successful audience reaction.

In this first section of *Effective Presentations* we will therefore discuss the chief elements that have to be weighed and worked out during the preparation of any presentation. The analysis covers oral and written presentations at the same time because the same planning applies to both. The word audience, in defiance of etymology, designates those at whom a presentation is directed, whether they hear it or read it.

Getting a presentation ready requires preliminary decisions on strategy. Before you do any work on any presentation, be sure you study the following aspects of your strategy.

First Ask These Six Questions

1. *Who are the audience?* This is an absolute first consideration, whether the audience listens or reads. Who are they in terms of their knowledge of the subject? In terms of power to make decisions? What is their self-interest in relation to the subject? What are their prejudices? What is their background of relationships with one another? With you? With the organization you represent?

Suppose you are an electrical engineer about to make a presentation about electrical insulating materials. What you know about your subject remains constant; how you get ready varies widely. Say your audience is electronics engineers. They require one approach. Purchasing agents require another. Your aim with electronics engineers is to secure professional acceptance of your data; with purchasing agents, it is to convince them that they should buy the materials you discuss. In one mixed audience the purchasing agents might be more important in deciding on the adoption of your materials; in another, it might be the engineers.

2. *Who makes the presentation?* The person first suggested to make a presentation is not always the one most suitable one to do it. Usually the audience expects the top-ranking person or the most knowledgeable one in a group to make a presentation. In some instances, the most skilled speaker in a group should present the main talk, and the most technically proficient one answer questions. Sometimes too many persons give parts of presentations, and the listeners grow confused or bored. Who talks or writes must be determined on the basis of who listens or reads and what has to be accomplished. An executive must often present material prepared by others, but he and his aides must think as one.

3. *When is the presentation? Do you have enough lead time?* The most common error made by the inexperienced communicator—and by the one who does not learn from experience—is to give himself too little time to get ready. The technical man often allows plenty of time for gathering data—that is his strong suit. Then he allows too little for preparing his presentation. He is less skilled at communication and slights what he does not like to do, or he does a good job of organizing a presentation and then ignores the rehearsal or rewriting.

4. *Where is the presentation to be given or printed? Under what circumstances?* The answers to these two questions have crucial bearing on getting a presentation ready. If it is oral, what will be the physical setup? For instance, will you be talking from a flat floor or from a platform? In someone's office or in a well-equipped conference room? At a scheduled meeting or at a pick-up lunch? If it is to be written, what publication is to print it? How many words will you be allowed?

5. *What is your controlling purpose?* The key to the strategy of your presentation is your controlling purpose. Your controlling purpose will usually fall into one of four categories: a) information, b) problem solving, c) persuasion, d) decision-making. It can always be put into one sentence—in effect, one of the following four: a) "We have completed the first phase of activity XYZ with the following results"; or b) "These seem the probable causes

of our problem, and these are some of the possible solutions"; or
c) "If you follow my suggestions, you will receive benefits R, S,
and T"; or d) "I recommend course of action Alpha rather than
Lambda or Omega for the following reasons."

You plan and execute a presentation so that your controlling
purpose sings out at all times. It does not matter how much you
know or how clever you are—if your audience is confused about
what you are driving at, your presentation has failed.

6. *How long should the presentation be?* How many presentations have you heard or read that were ruined because they
were too long? This does not mean that the shorter the presentations are, the better they are. It means that as you start getting
a presentation ready, you should estimate as accurately as possible how much time or space you will actually have. You may,
for instance, be told that you have an hour for an oral presentation. But if you are the fourth speaker on a morning program,
you may be called on a few minutes before noon and have to cut
your talk down to twenty minutes. If you are not on guard against
this common example of poor management of meetings, you are
in for a shock.

Whenever you have to make an important presentation, especially one for an unfamiliar audience or in unusual circumstances,
get the answers to all the questions you need for planning every
detail of your strategy. Later recheck every point. Often you turn
up significant differences the second time.

Audience Analysis Controls Your Strategy

No matter how well you know your subject, you always have
to make some adjustment in the details of your presentation
according to your analysis of the audience you address.

How often have you been confused by speakers and writers
who, for lack of briefing or indifference or because of a desire to
show off, have talked over your head? And how often have you
been irritated by others who for the same reasons have "talked
down," as if you knew nothing about a subject with which you
are well acquainted? If you do not know what you need to know
about your audience, find out. You can give a talk—say, a trave-

logue—to an audience you have not studied, but not a presentation.

Primarily, audience analysis means determining exactly the relationship between your purpose and the interests of the audience. Never forget that self-interest is the only audience interest you can count on with certainty.

Other audience factors have a bearing on oral presentations. How many persons will be in the audience? It is not uncommon to be told you have an audience of 100 and then to confront a scattered handful. Or to get the idea that you are going to have an informal office conversation and then find yourself standing in front of a roomful of people with notebooks.

Knowing who is in the audience can be of the utmost importance. For instance, suppose you make a presentation about a new metal alloy before a half-dozen company officers in a customer's plant and do not bother to find out who they are. You may strike out because you do not know that the research director, who is an authority in metallurgy, is present. Have someone give you a run-down on special members of an audience whenever your audience analysis suggests it is desirable.

It is easy to imagine that you know who your audience will be and then find you are mistaken. A magician once journeyed to a New England village to give a show to school children. Instead of being, as he had assumed, of high school age, the children were all little children. The magician had to leave out much of his show and improvise the rest with objects bought hastily from the 5 and 10.

One speaking engagement was painful for Dr. Benlowe and for his audience because he did not ask the right questions of the person who invited him to talk. He was told the audience was the P.T.A. of a school in the suburbs of the city to which he had just moved. Somehow he thought this meant a discussion group sitting around a table, and turned up prepared to moderate a discussion of the topic he had chosen to discuss—a philosophy of democracy. He walked into a big high school auditorium and found hundreds of adults wedged into tablet armchairs. They clearly expected a speech, and Dr. Benlowe was speechless.

Some months later Dr. Benlowe was invited to talk to another P.T.A. group in another suburb. He was told positively 150 would be there. He carefully prepared a formal speech. A storm came up and only 15 hardy souls turned out. They adjourned to a conference room and had a discussion around a table.

A psychologist was asked to talk on sales problems to 75 bond salesmen. Their company was having its annual summer sales meeting, and he was scheduled after dinner on the final evening. He was assured that a serious talk would be in order, and he did not bother to examine this premise closely. After five minutes it was apparent that the salesmen, having relaxed over cocktails for an hour before dinner and having eaten well, were in a mood to forget their problems, not to learn how to solve them. Either the presentation should have been scheduled for a regular working session, or the speaker should have been psychologist enough to prepare a shorter, lighter talk to fit the mood of the audience.

Angling a written presentation for individual readers and types of readers is an even more subtle matter. Reader analysis *must* precede composition.

Situation Analysis Shapes Your Attack

In order to achieve the purpose of your presentation, you must follow your audience analysis with an analysis of the situation. You must be clear about those factors in the total situation that will affect your success. Only through a study of these factors can you decide what points to stress and what evidence to choose to support your points. For instance, you can be sure that if you are asking your audience to spend money, they want two questions answered: How much? Is it worth it?

William Wickner, of William Wickner Associates, industrial designers, has been asked to present the capability of his firm to redesign the housemark of the Barr Wood Products Company. He holds preliminary conversations with the company's advertising agency, who have recommended a change and arranged for him to make the presentation.

Wickner learns that a schism exists in the management. The advertising manager and the sales manager want to give the company a new look. The president and the manufacturing vice president see no reason to change the old housemark, an ornate shield with three bars on it. The man in charge of packaging, who works for the manufacturing vice president, wants to modify the shield according to ideas he has worked out.

Wickner's strategy, he decides, is to try to earn the confidence of the entire group, not to try to make a win-or-lose single presentation. He may lose, but he believes it is more likely that he will lose if he tries to prove that the old symbol is now antiquated and difficult to use.

So in his first meeting he uses slides and a low-key exposition to present the philosophy he follows and a cross section of his work in graphics. He chooses samples of work he has done for national firms that the Barr management would have reason to know and respect. He gives names that they may consult. He does not criticize the old mark directly, but refers to the increasing number of consumer products of the company, the need for special appeals to women shoppers, and the new problems that arise in designing packages for hardware and other retail stores. He shows no eagerness to press for an immediate decision.

After another visit and individual talks with the management people, he wins first the support of the packaging man and then a contract for a new housemark, to be followed by its application to all company stationery, publications, and packages. His strategy —not to meet the underlying opposition head on—pays off.

Just because you have worked hard to prepare a budget or something of the sort does not entitle you to drag your audience over all the same ground, no matter how informal the occasion. They are looking only for what has significance in the context of the larger action situation.

One important factor in your situation analysis is your personal relation to the audience you are addressing and its probable reaction to you. This reaction may not be as much to you personally as to the subject; yet a negative reaction may be passed on to you. If the audience does not know much about your subject, you may well overcome a certain defensiveness by starting off with a simple illustration of what you are talking about. For instance, a distinguished eye surgeon when talking to laymen about detached retinas begins by comparing the retina to wallpaper. Then he continues to refer to this same homely, but apt image.

In any situation the hidden negative elements have to be countered. Sometimes when an audience does not know you, it will react to the stereotype suggested by something about you. Perhaps your dialect is different from that of your audience. This can set a group against you. A professor from the University of London with a cultivated British accent disarms his American audiences by saying, "I was brought up in a very poor section of London." This candor counteracts the stage stereotype of a British snob. But do not misread this example: He is candid, not apologetic.

Each speech situation presents its own variables. Two common hazards for professional speakers are a) to assume more technical knowledge than their listeners have and so to talk over their heads; b) to talk too much about technical details and too little about economic or other values of importance to the listeners. A good situation analysis will usually give you an "angle"—what line to take with a particular audience on a particular occasion.

Time Is Always a Critical Factor

Time, as already noted, is a critical factor in every presentation. It must always be considered in your situation analysis. If you have asked a busy man for "just five minutes" for an office presentation, say, and you need forty-five, you may not get started before the secretary announces the next appointment. Or you may overstay your time and make things rough for yourself and perhaps for your colleagues in the future.

You may think that you cannot do justice to your subject in the time allotted you. The trick of tailoring a presentation to a time limit is to make the interests of the audience, not the subject, the key to what you choose to discuss and what you treat fully while you skip over other aspects.

You might think that time would not be a hazard in written presentations, but it is. Publications specify length of articles, but you often have little to guide you in other areas, such as reports and memoranda. Then, too, you have no control over a reader's attention. Brevity, clarity, and interest are your chief helps.

Good strategy may lead you to postpone a presentation rather than try either to give it in a wholly inadequate amount of time or space, or to give it when the audience is distracted by another matter. This is particularly true if the audience is your boss.

Emotional Appeal Adds Another Dimension

Appeal to the emotions of an audience is often the most decisive strategic element in a presentation. The inexperienced writer or speaker may overlook this element entirely. It may seem to him to have no relevance to the subject or the occasion. Yet it is probably not extreme to say that emotion has a place in planning the strategy of every presentation.

For instance, you might think that a chemist presenting a report on a scientific breakthrough to his colleagues would have little use for emotional appeal of any kind. Yet scientists say that they are more inclined to share a fellow scientist's estimate of the importance of his work if he shows enthusiasm and conviction about it. They also say that they are more willing to heed his request for their help, if he sounds sincere and potentially grateful.

Most of us can swallow an extraordinary amount of flattery without any ill effects whatever. Recognition of any virtues the audience may have in relation to your subject, such as their technical knowledge, their pride in doing good work, or their fair-mindedness, is only courtesy, not flattery. Deciding on such details is part of getting your presentation ready.

Let us say that you have to present the final recommendations of a consulting firm to the officers of a company. Some of your findings are critical of the way the officers have handled their affairs. Your chief recommendation will result in changes that will redistribute the responsibilities of some of the officers. Getting ready both your written report and the oral presentation that accompanies its submission would anticipate a negative reaction from these men. You would try to neutralize that emotional response. You might stress how much these officers had contributed to the analysis of their problems, the high potential growth of the company, and how great the rewards will be if that potential can be realized.

Without such emotional appeals—which need not be crudely

put, by the way—your presentation might be lucid and logical. Yet the resentment of the negatively affected officers might lead to a vigorous attack on your recommendations. The president might nullify your whole effort by compromising, merely to keep the peace. Or he might file your report.

A logical presentation shows to its best advantage when it glows with the appropriate emotional appeals. They should be thought out as a standard part of the planning strategy.

3

Organizing Your Material

Once you have analyzed your audience and the situation attending your presentation, you are ready to organize your material—but not until. It is amazing how few executives—men of unquestioned competence in their field—know how to go about organizing any presentation besides a routine one in a familiar specialized area. All too often they experience three kinds of trouble. First, they spend far too much time raking their material together. Second, the material does not fit the audience as well as it should. Third, it is hard to follow.

In this chapter we will go over some exceedingly simple suggestions about your first moves toward giving your material form. As in chess, only if you make the first moves systematically, can you hope to proceed in an orderly fashion.

The Solitaire System Simplifies Analysis

Planning by 3 x 5 cards is the fastest way to analyze a topic and to arrive at a logical arrangement of a presentation. Sit down with a fresh pack of 3 x 5 cards and jot down what you consider your key ideas. When you can think of no more, start sorting the cards into packs according to relatedness. Often this is good enough for a start. With an unfamiliar subject, you may take notes for weeks or months.

Any subject can be arranged in a few major divisions. It is no exaggeration to say that you are not ready to make a presentation until you can outline it on one 3 x 5 card. You can then organize your cards in subdivisions. As you do this, you will catch duplications and think of major points that you have omitted.

The virtue of this solitaire system is the speed with which you can analyze and organize even a complex subject. To sit down and write out an entire presentation, or even an outline, consecutively out of your head is to do the job the slow, hard way—the poor way. Revisions are then psychologically and physically difficult to make. They take a long time. Cards can be shuffled in seconds.

Another advantage of cards is that you can throw one away when you think of a better idea or a better phrasing. Because you put only a few key words on cards, the solitaire system fosters the habit of essential thinking and lessens self-confusion.

Isolate Your Controlling Purpose

Your controlling purpose is your message—the essence of what you are going to say. It is your topic plus a summary statement about it. The title of your presentation may be "Psychology in the Foundry Industry." Your controlling purpose may be "Psychology cannot solve the economic problems of the foundry industry, but it can help with its human problems." Because of the importance of your controlling purpose, you should write it down as soon as possible, check it carefully, and then base your planning on it.

This difference between a topic and a controlling purpose is one of the most critical single points in planning presentations—and in the success or failure of your effort. Failure to say to yourself, This is precisely what I want to say; this is my message; this is what I want them to do, results in a lack of direction.

Without a clear purpose to control your progress, you wander like a child in a daisy field. With a clear purpose, everything you say has a reason. Without a controlling purpose, you gather and present, possibly interesting, but poorly related information and ideas. The audience is confused as you go along. They fail to add up what you have said so as to respond as you wish. How can they? You have not figured it out yourself.

You will often have two controlling purposes—that which you express and a private one. This duality need not be as deceitful as it sounds. For instance, in the hypothetical talk above, a consulting psychologist might be critical of what foundrymen expect psychology to do and yet select and accent his material in the hope of being retained as a consultant.

Patient trial drafts to get a precise statement of your controlling purpose can save much patching, hacking, and muddling. A clear statement of purpose does more than give direction and goal to your presentation. It indicates to you what must be included. As you go about getting together the material indicated, you will often see that you have to limit the scope of the presentation. That is the only way to do justice to what is most essential to your purpose. Trying to cover too much ground is a common weakness of amateur presentations.

Clearly, you cannot write a meaningful statement of purpose without thinking hard about the triangular relation between A, the audience, S, the subject, and you. Suppose that you are a mining engineer appearing before a group of bankers to borrow capital to begin silver mining operations in South America. Your analysis of S alone might lead you to draft a controlling purpose something like this: "The Dulcimer Silver Mine is a good investment for you because the silver is abundant and of excellent quality." But when you analyze A, you might add "and because the high price of silver, low cost of operations, and stable political conditions promise a quick pay-back."

In other words, no matter what your interest in the subject may be, the controlling purpose of your presentation takes into account the interest of your audience in that subject. In the instance given, your purpose would include dealing with the three questions bankers would want answered after receiving your assurance about the amount and quality of the silver.

Establish a 1-2-3 Pattern

As stated already, most presentations can be organized under
three to five main headings. They must be if an audience is to remember clearly what has been said. Too many presentations follow a freight-car sort of pattern—one point after another in a long
series. As soon as you think yourself compelled to present, say,
ten different major ideas, analyze them again. You will probably
find that they fall together in associated groups. All of history
can be summed up under ancient, medieval, and modern; surely
the material that goes into an hour or half-hour presentation can
be brought under the simple analysis of a few key words.

Patterns are usually determined by purpose. The inherent logic
of most subjects will give you a basic progression. A headquarters
report on a tour of inspection of a number of military installations,
for example, could be organized geographically. Or it might follow the simplest of all patterns, the *chronological*—the sequence
of installations visited and then the summary of findings. The step-
by-step progression is the most common 1-2-3 pattern for explanatory presentations, especially for technical ones.

Often an abstract subject has no obvious chronological sequence, yet a time pattern can be imposed on it: 1) Darwin's
early ideas about evolution were extremely tentative. 2) Through
the years after his trip to South America he gradually clarified
them as theories. 3) Later in his life he retreated somewhat to
placate critics because some of the evidence he needed to support
his theories was still lacking.

A chronological pattern is not only easy for an audience to
follow. It helps the person making a presentation to remember
what comes after what.

The *analytical* 1-2-3 pattern may yield as simple an organization as that of a general idea either divided into its parts or illustrated by specific applications. Or it might follow a problem-to-
solution progression: 1) statement of problem, 2) hypotheses
about its solution, 3) tests of hypotheses, 4) results.

Another basic pattern of organization is the *comparison*. For
executive presentations it is standard because making a choice
between two or more possible courses of action comes close to

summing up what executives "do." The 1-2-3 pattern may be something like this: 1) the advantages and disadvantages of alternative A, 2) the advantages and disadvantages of alternative B, 3) why alternative B is preferable. Another standard comparative pattern is the review of data such as sales to date compared with estimated sales and with actual sales of the previous year.

Sometimes you will also find it desirable to observe a *psychological* progression. You will proceed from the easy to the difficult, from matters of immediate interest to those that are more remote, and from areas of agreement to areas of differences of opinion or downright opposition. In other words, you work from a base of acceptance to matters that are more difficult for the audience to understand or to agree to. Confusion, misunderstanding, or hostility at the beginning of a presentation is a heavy handicap.

No presentation technique is more basic than organizing your material into a simple 1-2-3 pattern of key ideas that expand a clear controlling purpose.

Collect Relevant Data

Lining up facts to support your ideas seems obvious enough. Yet often a presentation is weak because the speaker depends on assertion. He does not offer the kind of evidence that clinches what he has alleged is true. Again, audience analysis and situation analysis come into play. For a particular audience or situation, certain data will be more relevant, better understood, and more convincing than other equally valid data.

In talking to a meeting of motor rewind men, an electrical engineer would offer insulation data about the sort of motors they deal with, not some other kind. They would understand his evidence and be more likely to believe that the insulation he recommends would help them make higher profits.

With varying degrees of thoroughness all presentations require some sort of research. You may be reporting the results of years of study of how molecules whose structure is similar to that of molecules present in cancer cells might be used to block the growth of cancer cells. Or you may merely search your memory for evidence from novels and plays you have read to support your belief that contemporary literature is nihilistic.

The important thing to remember is that the data supporting your key ideas must be relevant, not merely true. Relevance is determined by the influence the evidence will have on your audience in the light of a) their interest in the subject and b) how you want to influence them.

Suppose you are presenting a report on cancer cells to a group of cancer specialists. You would use only scientific data because the specialists would understand what you were doing. For a lay audience you would have to back up to include information about the structure of molecules. You would have to use models or drawings of molecules for them; whereas you would need only the formulas of the chemical structures for medical specialists.

Similarly, the same controlling purpose about the nihilism of contemporary literature would require the selection of different authors, novels, and plays for different audiences. Six French writers might be familiar to a group of college professors; three to a group of college students; and none to a women's literary club. Not to be boorish, you would search for novels and plays that your undergraduates and women's club members might be expected to have heard of, if not read or seen.

The selection of relevant data is often more subtle than in these examples. But even these examples would in reality offer choices that would have to be weighed. One audience might contain a professor highly enthusiastic about the work of Genet, for instance, and you would have to discuss Genet's work tactfully. On the other hand, you might decide that a women's club would find detailed discussion of Genet embarrassing, and so you would limit yourself to generalizations, or you might not mention him at all. In many presentations you have a wide range of possible data, and you can strengthen your effect on your audience by wise selection.

Examples Add Clarity, Color, and Credibility

Unrelieved analytical statements are hard for an audience to understand, to keep interested in, and to remember. Facts and

figures used as supporting evidence do much to offset the forget-
tability of continued assertion as well as its lack of credibility.
After wise choice of relevant data, your best means of helping
your audience to understand what you are driving at is the example. An example does not necessarily prove—it makes clear.
It does more; it adds color, and it adds credibility.

What the example does is to translate the general to the specific. Perhaps more than that, it translates the impersonal to the
personal. A discussion of the English educational system soon
becomes confusing as you enumerate the various unfamiliar clas-
sifications of schools. Your audience would find it clearer and
more interesting if you gave examples: "My cousin's son Derek,
for example, earned high grades in the national examination given
all students about their eleventh year. He was able to go to a high
school specializing in science and is now following an electronic
engineering curriculum at Sussex University. On the other hand,
my cousin's daughter Hetty wanted to be a secretary. After her
eleventh-year examination, she followed a completely different
course . . ."

The example usually stands as typical of others in some sort of
series. A variant is the anecdote. It is both personal and narrative
in form. "Once, when I was in England, I visited a school for
boys who had failed the national test and were therefore not
going to a high school to prepare for a university . . ."

Another variant is the personal reference. This might take the
form of saying "I thought that you might like to hear what I
learned last summer about the English educational system." Or
you might say, "Tom Harrow, an English exchange student who
was here last year, has written me the following . . ." Or you might
inject: "We have as a guest today Joan Dodd, who was an exchange student in England last year. Perhaps Joan will give her
observations later."

Examples, anecdotes, and personal references can also help gain
credence for your ideas. Having been in England and observed
the English educational system firsthand, does not make you an
authority, but your references to this experience add credibility
to what you are saying. The examples of your cousin's son and
daughter help your audience to *realize*—that is, to enter into and

comprehend—the actualities of the English system. They therefore believe what you are saying as they might not otherwise do.

Examples, anecdotes, and personal references *personalize* your
presentation and make it more comprehensible, memorable, colorful, and believable. These interpolations should seem spontaneous
—and may be. But since you know that such concreteness is necessary, you should gather what you need in advance and place it
where it will pick up your presentation. Such material adds sea-
soning to the food you are offering your audience. Since this illustrative material also contributes to the acceptance of your ideas
by the audience, it must be selected with an eye to its relevance
and believability, just as your data are.

Plan Audio-Visual Aids from the Start

As you are organizing your presentation—the communication
problem you are facing, not just the intellectual one presented
by your material—jot down suggestions for using graphics and
other audio-visual aids. (See Part II.) Since audio-visual aids are
a significant part of most presentations, they are an intrinsic part
of your planning. In fact, you will often do well *first* to make up
your chart or slide material or whatever other aid you use (so
long as it plays a basic role in your presentation) and *then* decide
what you will say afterwards.

This sequence is a much-neglected piece of common sense. The
result is often that a speaker or writer is needlessly perplexed.
He has fixed in his mind that he must say or write material better
communicated by his audio-visual aids. When you start with your
graphics and other aids, it may also give you a tighter 1-2-3 pattern than if you write and then develop the aids. And you will
save time. You will usually be forced to come to grips at once
with what is essential in your presentation, instead of fiddling
around gathering more and more data.

In organizing a presentation built around a substantial number
of slides or a motion picture, you will find a preliminary *story
board* useful. It is simply a series of cards or sheets of paper, each
of which combines a one-sentence statement of a key idea and
a rough sketch of the photograph or drawing needed to illustrate

it. Sometimes the illustrative material may already exist. Then the words indicate what should be said about it. You may need experienced help in roughing out a story board, but see what you can do yourself. You will find that this simplified approach helps you enormously to organize a presentation that is conceived largely in visual terms.

4

Developing the Presentation

After you have collected and organized your material, you are ready to develop the presentation proper. Here you bring to bear your realization that a presentation is, in effect, an art form. The nature of your material, your purpose, the interests of your audience, and circumstances in which it is to be given all have a bearing on the form your presentation takes.

You may, for instance, be going to make a presentation to a small group after a lunch at which you are host. It is important not to give the impression that you are trying to sell anything. Your material otherwise might be more effectively communicated in a formal presentation with graphic aids. But you develop it into a hand-in-pocket understressed talk—perhaps you do not even stand up.

What Form Should Your Presentation Take— Oral or Written?

Sometimes the choice of whether to make an oral presentation or a written one needs thinking over. For instance, scores of candidates for jobs have been passed over because the potential employer had only a letter of application to go on. Had circumstances—or the candidates' determination to get the job—permitted face-to-face presentation of their qualifications, some would certainly have been hired. The chance to convey information and impressions not conveyable by mail would have made the difference. On the other hand, most professors squander a considerable part of their lives making oral presentations of involved factual and analytical matter that might be much better put into the students' hands in written form for careful reading, analysis, and future reference.

The combination of oral and written presentations is often desirable. Suppose you are going to appear before a city council to argue against one rezoning proposal and in favor of another. If you make only an oral presentation, with maps and charts, you depend on the memories of each member (a faulty instrument) if the decision is postponed until the next meeting. If, however, each member can take away with him a written brief of your presentation, which you have prepared in advance, the probability of his understanding, and thus agreeing with your objections and counter proposal, is heightened.

The decision about whether to make an oral or a written presentation, or to combine the two, really goes back to the realization that you *are* making a presentation—that is, that the stakes in the situation warrant your taking special pains to put your message across. The colloquialism "put across" indicates the common realization of the dynamic effort necessary to span the gulf between the facts and ideas churning in one mind and their acceptance by others.

Take the illustration just given, a letter of application for a job. The applicant's career will be affected by the outcome. Yet many such letters are written hastily, leave essential questions unanswered, and are marred by errors corrected or not corrected. Many more do not create a favorable impression because they are dull.

It takes a certain amount of imagination, or perhaps plain seriousness of purpose, to realize when a communication situation is sufficiently important to call for careful preparation that is the mark of a good presentation. Understanding that a situation does call for a presentation should bring about the sort of analysis that will determine what form it should take.

Should You Write a Script for an Oral Presentation?

Should you write out a presentation that is to be given orally? The question is a personal one. Some speakers never use notes even. Some use notes only. Some use a carefully written script to establish in their mind the pattern of the material and the key ideas and phrases, then they ignore the script entirely. Others write out a complete script and then reduce it to notes. They use key phrases as their guide. Others follow a written script closely, but appear not to do so. Many, too many, think that reading a script, no matter how badly, *is* making a presentation.

For many speakers a script becomes a straitjacket. They keep trying to remember what they wrote and fail to communicate directly and convincingly with the audience. Reading is always indirect communication—the speaker seems openly to admit that his authority rests in the script, not in his mind.

As always, the final arbiters are the situation, you, and the audience. Sometimes what you say is to be published, and you have to write it anyway. Sometimes the occasion is so formal that the style of formal prose is appropriate. In the normal use of the word "presentation," this situation rarely occurs.

A busy executive, such as a high government official, often has to give many important presentations—to Congressional committees, for instance. He cannot have intimate knowledge of the details of each one, let alone get them ready from the ground up himself. In such a case a staff-prepared script, carefully studied and underlined and safely organized in a looseleaf notebook, is excellent insurance for an experienced speaker. After adequate rehearsal, he needs only to flip the pages and flick his eye over the copy. He then recalls the drift of what he is to say at each point and picks up statistical material keyed to his charts.

In practice, presentations far too often are based on written scripts. Ideally, nothing matches the dialogue that takes place between the full mind of the master of the subject and the well-informed and interested audience. This ideal situation exists only occasionally. The nearest approach for you is to master your thoroughly prepared material to such an extent that you can talk it fluently without dependence on script, notes, or charts.

In most normal presentation situations, if you cannot talk freely from note cards or charts, you do not know your subject well enough to talk at all. Much of the answer to the initial question about writing or not writing out a presentation may lie in the next section on graphics and other aids.

A Good Lead Creates a Favorable Climate

Your first remarks are your "lead"—your attention-getter. Do not assume that your lead must be a joke that would be appropriate in opening an after-dinner talk. Often presentations do not go over because speakers try to use after-dinner tactics in inappropriate situations. A modest business-like opening can be much more effective than a lugged-in funny story, particularly if the audience has already heard the story. Planning your first seemingly impromptu remarks can create a favorable climate for your entire presentation.

If circumstances seem to call for some graceful remarks before you get down to business, talk about your audience or their environment. Never talk about yourself if you can help it, except modestly to identify yourself with your audience. Never talk about your preparation for the occasion or mention other audiences to whom you have made the same presentation. Your audience and situation analysis should give you something pleasant and positive that you can plan to say at the outset. Try to avoid hackneyed leads like how-glad-I-am-to-be-in-this-great-city and what-a-privilege etc., etc.

If you do not have a fresh, sincere opening prepared, try to find something usable after you arrive on the scene of your presentation. Ask questions and keep your ears open. You can often pick up timely personal references this way, such as, "Mr. Morgan has been telling me what a great job Ralph Van Buren and the Economic Development Council have been doing to attract new industry to the Valley." Then, with ingenuity, you can build a bridge to what you are going to talk about. Such a lead has spontaneity and a personal flavor.

Identify, Reassure, and Orient the Audience

Early in your presentation plan to let your audience know that you are aware of who they are, what they know and do, and why they are interested in your subject.

In a talk before a meeting of motor rewind men, you might begin by saying how long your company had been doing business with them. You might also mention the names of people you had worked with personally. If you are discussing labor relations in the foundry industry, you might reassure an audience of foundrymen by naming their critical problems right away and indicating what efforts you have made to understand those problems.

Knowing your audience and knowing what you want them to believe, you should include an audience tie-in from time to time as you go along. The number of such references will vary considerably with the situation. A technical talk before a scientific society normally has none or few. Nevertheless, there is no law against relating even a scientific talk to a particular audience. Any presentation before a civic organization ought to offer several opportunities for tying in your material with the known interests of the group.

The tie-in is not a cynical device for manipulating an audience in your favor. To use material clearly not designed for the audience you are addressing may be flagrantly discourteous. Your tie-in indicates that a connection exists. As in the case of examples, such relating of your material to the audience should seem natural and spontaneous. But, again, the professional presenter knows in advance that he has to tie his audience into his presentation, and he automatically looks for opportunities as part of organizing his material.

In a written presentation you sometimes do not have either the same need or opportunity to identify the audience precisely. An editorial in a newspaper advocating rejection of a piece of legislation is supposed to appeal to the entire public. But a report on such legislation written by a professor of economics for a property-owners' association probably would identify these readers explicitly throughout.

Beyond identifying your audience at the beginning, you have to orient and reassure them—bring them into focus with your subject, and reduce fear or hostility that may be present. This usually takes the form of reminding them of the importance that the subject has for them. Often this relationship escapes them. Your function is to help them by analyzing the material from their point of view. For instance, a presentation to office workers in a plant about cost reduction might get a ho-hum reaction unless the speaker stresses the direct relation between cost of operations, sales, profits, and the pay and fringe benefits of the persons listening to him.

Brief introductory focusing is also necessary to drive other subjects out of the listeners' minds and prepare them for your material. Immediate launching into your main material may cause half your audience to miss some key terms and ideas and so remain confused about the whole presentation.

Orienting the audience requires that you immediately clarify any obvious questions about your topic. For instance, suppose you are making a presentation to business executives about the topic "Management by Objectives." The inevitable question in their minds will be—how does this method differ from the way we have been managing our businesses? If you do not dispose of this key question at the outset, they will not be properly oriented. They may only half listen to you while they wait for clarification, or think up a devastating speech to make as soon as they get a chance. If no quick clarification is forthcoming, your audience may reject your entire case.

You often use this relating of the subject to the audience to create an emotional appeal at the outset. This develops interest and an inclination toward agreement with what you will present later.

In negotiations or talks on sensitive subjects, your audience may imagine that you are going to say something unacceptable to them and be unjustifiably hostile. Here again is where audience analysis and situation analysis are vital. As far as possible, you must disarm opposition at the outset. You must plan in advance

what you can say that will prevent misunderstanding and antagonism. This requires intimate knowledge of your audience. Talking to several people who know a specific audience better than
you do, is part of readying a presentation that will be reassuring
to that audience.

Maintain the 1-2-3 Pattern

Much of the success of your presentation proper depends on
how well you maintain your 1-2-3 pattern in the minds of your
listeners or readers. Once you have established your controlling
purpose and main steps, everything you do from there on should
contribute to a unified response. Your presentation should build
up to an inevitable conclusion, not run down and peter out.

It is usually desirable to tell your audience what main points
you are going to touch on and how you will conduct your presentation. Too many meetings take place without a clear understanding as to whether they are informational, problem-solving, persuasive, or decision-making.

A written presentation generally should follow the same policy
of sketching in the pattern at the outset. This may be done with
a sentence or two or, as in technical-paper presentations, with an
abstract.

Indicate your time limit and what you plan to do about questions or future action. If you expect the audience to do anything
—whether you are giving a talk to six colleagues in an office or to
600 people in an auditorium—make clear at the outset what you
want them to do. Sometimes, of course, you may hold back precisely what you want them to do until you have motivated them
to want to do it.

Poor timing, particularly by talking or writing too long, is one
of the most common ways of obscuring the total pattern and
ruining the impact of your presentation. Another is digressing;
another is over-subtle complexity of thought.

The binder. The hardest presentation to give is one that deals
primarily with ideas. It is harder for the audience to follow
abstractions that are connected only by logic than, say, the steps
in a process. Thus it is desirable to look around at the beginning

of your preparation for a unifying device. Such a device is sometimes called a binder.

President Franklin Roosevelt, in order to explain to the American people the complex reasons for our help to the Allies, spoke
about his neighbor's house being on fire. A business writer to explain a fresh idea about the kind of person a successful entrepre-
neur is, coins a deliberately unusual phrase, "veridical percep-
tion," the act of recognizing people, things, or situations as they
really are.

Another business writer to explain a concept of the future importance of the production man in management divides the history
of the role of production into three phases. We are now entering
the third, he says. These devices catch the attention of the audience and through repetition bind the presentation together.

Transitions. Just as one of the marks of the pro among short-
stops is how fast he gets rid of the ball, so skilful handling of
transitions is one mark of the pro among presentation-makers.
Transitions are the bridges from one point to another. Some con-
nect items; some, major sections. In writing, the connecting function is uppermost. In an oral presentation, the separating function
is just as important.

An experienced speaker or writer directs as much of his attention to his transitions as he does to any element of his presentations. How do I get from here to there? he thinks. If I bring this
matter in at this point, how do I tie it to what goes before and
comes after?

The danger in an oral presentation is that the audience will
not know when you have finished Item G and are starting on
Item H, or when you have finished Item H and are starting on
Item I. Suppose you are discussing a manufacturing problem in
Item G. Your transition to Item H might be: "This problem can
be better understood by a brief historical account of factory operations from Eli Whitney to Henry Ford." Then you might block
off Item H and bridge to Item I by a transitional remark such as:
"With this factory background in mind, let us turn to what has
happened in marketing."

Make the major divisions stand apart from one another by

signals—"Let's take up the second point . . ." "You will be interested in what we are doing with closed-circuit TV." Then you will not say monotonously: "My next point is . . ."; "Next slide, please."

Conveying to a listening audience a blueprint of your controlling purpose and main ideas is no easy task. In your planning, therefore, you should plant cues to warn yourself of the major divisions, so that you can signal the audience by a variety of stimulating vocal means. Large red crayon marginal numbers are a simple way of reminding yourself that you are taking up a new major section. You might also mark in your notes those points in your talk that you can skip if you have to. Charts and slides should be adequate reminders of major shifts, but often they seem not to be.

In a written presentation you rely on typographical effects, captions, and paragraphing, as well as on signal words, phrases, and sentences.

Facts Do Not Speak for Themselves

Joe Walker, a lawyer in a tobacco company, is asked to present to the law school seniors of his university the case for a career in the legal department of a corporation. He feels strongly that he has a message. When the time comes, he gets up without notes and launches into an account of what he does and what sort of company he works for. Knowing that the students have no reason to be familiar with the intricacies of the tobacco business, he stops to explain in detail how his company was founded, its history, and its operations. The students are bored. He talks about his own work in such a way that he seems to be setting himself up as a model of success. The students are repelled. The presentation is a failure.

Joe stubbed his toe at the beginning of his presentation. What he left out was the indication to the audience of what his facts signified. What he neglected to say was something like this: "I have been given the assignment of presenting to you seniors a case for a career in the legal department of a company as distinct from private practice and government service. I will illustrate my points by reference to my own company and my own career because they are the ones I know. Tobacco is a pretty specialized kind of business, and I'll have to explain some of the work we do in our department. But essentially I think you will find much the same opportunities in the legal department of any corporation." Brief references from time to time to this statement would have guided the students and reminded Joe that the facts about his company and his career were merely illustrative, not significant in themselves.

One of the commonest ways of losing an audience is through an over-abundance of facts and too little statement of the inferences to be drawn from them. In a talk where you are making recommendations, it is well to follow a logical FIR plan—Facts, Inferences, Recommendations. It is a common fault to switch from the statement of facts to recommendations without covering the logically important step of the inferences. The facts given may be true but not justify the unstated inferences on which the recommendations are silently based. If you do not draw the inferences from the facts, the audience probably will not. They may therefore miss the connection between the main part of your presentation and your recommendations. They may then reject your recommendations.

A salesman has not made a good presentation when he says to a shipbuilder, in effect: F) "Dur-Seel is expensive, but is the only permanent flexible waterproof marine caulk on the market. It is the easiest to apply, and it can be applied equally well in cold or hot weather." R) "You ought to specify Dur-Seel for all your ships." He needs to include the intermediate step, the inferences to be drawn from the facts. I) "In the long run Dur-Seel is the cheapest marine caulk because it has the lowest labor costs. Unskilled labor can apply it in any working weather. Unlike other caulks, it does not have to be replaced; therefore it involves no further labor costs." The recommendation gets its strength from the inferences, not from the starting facts.

The usual reason for the dropped inference is that the person making the presentation is full of his subject. He thinks his conclusions follow overwhelmingly from the evidence he has presented. This is a dangerous assumption. He may go further—he may even neglect to state his conclusions because he thinks them self-evident too.

You need to steer the thinking of your listeners or readers through these three FIR steps—Facts, Inferences, Recommendations. Nailing down the inferences to be drawn from the facts you present is what persuades an audience that your recommendations are inevitable.

Here is a statement in a reputable textbook: "It is true that *ain't* has made an appearance in the controversial third edition of *Webster's New International Dictionary,* but try using it seriously in a business letter or report and see what the reaction is!" This is an example of misleading handling of facts and inferences.

It is a fact that *ain't* appears in the third edition of Merriam's *Webster's Third International Dictionary.* But the essential fact of what this dictionary says about the word is withheld, though the discrediting adjective *controversial* is included. The skipped inference makes this seemingly straightforward statement unintentionally dishonest. The inference is that, if a word appears in a dictionary, it has received the stamp of approval for use on all occasions. This inference is false. Dictionaries merely record usage. They do not determine what it should be, and they are at pains to indicate exact levels of usage. (See chapter 15.)

In this instance the Merriam editors record that the word is more common in less educated speech, that certain forms are substandard, but that certain other forms, especially *ain't I*, are, in fact, used *orally* by many cultivated speakers. Such factual reporting is a far cry from sanctioning *ain't* for any use, let alone for formal business writing.

Logical Reasoning Underlies Sound Presentations

The soundness of any presentation is based on the logical reasoning that lies beneath the surface. Reasoning, therefore, is the most important element in developing the material that you collect. Reasoning, the psychologists have decided, is the same thing as problem solving. I once wrote a book called *The Art of Problem Solving,* which you might look up. Here are a few key ideas to help you:

The danger of assumptions. All reasoning is based on assumptions of some sort—something like Euclid's axioms that you accept as true when you start to solve a plane geometry problem. Right here is the source of most of the large troubles in this world as well as of our own small difficulties. How much more attainable world peace would be if the communists, nationalists, and racists were to question the assumptions on which they base their aggressions.

From the time you first plan your presentation until your final rehearsal, you must ask yourself two questions: What assumptions am I taking for granted? Are they true?

In a certain research organization government contracts were never sought because everyone "knew" that the government does not permit exclusive patents on research for which it contracts. Then one day someone questioned the assumption and went to Washington to talk with Defense Department officials. He found that, while the assumption is true in certain kinds of research, it is not true in others. His company soon began submitting bids and has since been awarded several hundred thousand dollars of research contracts. It had cost the company over the years not only a rich harvest of contracts but also the opportunity to carry on research in areas that it could not finance itself—all because the officers of the company took for granted as wholly true an assumption that was only partly true.

Assuming that something is so when it is not is the cause of most of our troubles. But beyond simple errors of fact, how do you know when something is true? You have two distinct situations. You can sometimes prove by test, calculation, or observation that something is *invariably true*—that the boiling point of water varies with atmospheric pressure, for example. At other times you can only build a case for believing that something is *probably* true.

Since the daily business of executives is making decisions about actions with future consequences, establishing the reliability of inferences concerning probability is a major aim of professional presentations. At some point in many of your presentations you will seek to establish that one choice of several possibilities is more *desirable* than the others.

Behind such presentations is always a great deal of sophisticated thinking. To hope to give successful presentations, therefore, without understanding the elements of logical reasoning is like hoping to be a concert pianist without reading music.

Five Ways to Establish Probability

There are five common ways to try to establish degrees of probability: a) by association, b) by analogy, c) by authority, d) by instances, and e) by causal relation. You use all of these methods of reasoning habitually. They are all as fraught with danger as a TV Western.

Of these methods only instances and causal relations are reliable instruments of logical reasoning. Nevertheless, we all use association, analogy, and authority to reach conclusions and to bolster up their plausibility.

Association. If a scientist finds cobalt in fields where healthy cows pasture and none in fields where cows are not healthy, he may reason that the association of cobalt and the health of cows is significant. Until he checks this observation in a laboratory, he has merely established a plausible hypothesis, not proof. The Hymettus Candy Company always has had high profits when car sales are high. This year the sale of cars is at an all-time high. Hymettus may do well, but this association has none of the dependability of cobalt and cows or crocuses and robins.

Analogy. Analogy is one of the most natural ways of reasoning. A savage is caught in a thunder storm. The tree he stands under is struck by lightning. When next lightning begins to flash, he hides in a cave. Here is a sound bit of reasoning by analogy. But again, the fact that the circumstances are similar does not mean that the same events will take place. A score of book publishers may grow successful by mergers; if publishers Black and White merge, they will not necessarily be successful.

Since experience is largely made up of analogies, analogy has its place in all our reasoning. Yet it never proves; it only suggests plausible possibilities.

Authority. If a county agent had to convince a dairyman that he should add cobalt to the diet of his cattle, he might show him a publication of the Department of Agriculture recommending the procedure. He would be increasing the plausibility that his recommendation would work by calling on authority.

Clearly, the usefulness of this device rests largely on the degree of credence the audience places in the authority cited.

Association, analogy, and authority cannot establish certainty, but when their limitations are understood, they are fruitful aids to reasoning.

Instances. The method of instances is different. It is a routine scientific procedure to prove that one solution of a problem is correct because in repeated tests it always works. But in human affairs the variables are so great that the instances cannot be added up with certainty. The fact that the city manager plan has been a success in a hundred cities does not prove that it will be in Center City, Iowa. Yet successful instances are certainly relevant, and they are the most convincing evidence you can possibly cite, if you are recommending the city manager plan for Center City.

The degree of probability adduced by the use of instances varies with circumstances. Once an atomic bomb was detonated, or the sound barrier was broken by a plane, or a man stepped out of a space capsule and floated, no further proof was necessary. These things can be done and can be duplicated as often as desired, though not without the possibility of mechanical failure. Once a new vaccine seems to have beneficial effects, however, hundreds of controlled tests have to be run before the probability of its successful use can be accepted. Even then individual exceptions often take place, and side effects may occur in time.

In many situations you will commonly use an instance to support an assertion without claiming that it proves your generalization. Zero Cryogenics is a good company to invest in. Mr. Heiss bought some of its stock, and the stock doubled in value in two years. The single instance can be highly convincing if a potential investor knows Mr. Heiss and respects his judgment about investments. In such a sales situation, however, several instances of investors who made out well would be even more convincing.

Cause and effect. Cause and effect relations are the backbone of scientific and legal proof. A scientist did prove by laboratory tests that cobalt does in fact cause beneficial effects in the diet of cows.

Reasoning based on causal relations goes two ways—from cause to effect and effect to cause. The difference is a matter of time. In the first you reason that A *will cause* B. In the second, that B must *have been caused* by A. When an advertising manager presents his budget, he argues that if he puts $100,000 into advertising product Y, he will help meet the sales goals for that product. If the goals are met, he will argue that the $100,000 in advertising had a decisive effect. In both of these instances the reasoning is probably valid, but, again, it is not inevitably so.

The catch in all causal relations reasoning is that only under the strictest scientific conditions does one phenomenon inevitably cause another or is one event inevitably caused by only one cause. Maybe $50,000 of advertising would be as effective as $100,000. Maybe the success of this particular sales campaign was largely due to a new use of product Y by the sales efforts of one distributor.

Since most problems of management are resolved almost wholly on the basis of judgments about probability, your presentations are valuable in proportion to the care with which you are scrupulous about your methods of reasoning.

Strengthen Your Endings in Four Ways

The ending is usually the least well-planned part of any presentation. Yet it may be the most important part. Four points should be reviewed as you plan your ending.

Summary. A clear summary of your controlling purpose and your main points can make sure that your listeners get the big picture. A good summary is a fresh statement of your case with repetition of key words previously used. Without such a restatement, your listeners may go away with a jumble of details obscuring main ideas. Some of them may even imagine that you said the reverse of what you did say.

For instance, the salesman might sum up his presentation to a shipbuilder like this: "In the long run, Mr. Bowditch, you will increase your profits by using Dur-Seel. Dur-Seel will do a better job than any other caulk on the market because it is the only permanent flexible waterproof marine caulk. It will reduce your labor costs because unskilled labor can apply it; it can be applied in any working weather; and it will practically never have to be replaced during the life of a ship."

Recommendations. If your presentation includes a recommendation, particularly one requiring action on the part of the audience, state it clearly as part of your ending. Do not assume that, because you have mentioned a certain course of action, you can wind up with a vague, "I hope you agree with me that this is a good thing to do." Plan the precise words you will use in your recommendations.

The salesman has not planned his presentation to the shipbuilder properly unless he says something like: "I'm going to leave you a gallon sample of Dur-Seel free, Mr. Bowditch. You use it. Then I'll be back next week to take your order for ten drums because I know you'll want that much for these three cabin cruisers you're building."

Emotional appeal. If your talk is aimed at arousing an emotional reaction, plan how this appeal may be strongly put in your conclusion. A talk about cost reduction to plant workers might end: "Cooperation in cutting costs is the best way you can safeguard your job and your fringe benefits and make pay raises possible."

Exit line. Your planning should always include an exit line. You have often observed a speaker floundering around at the end of his talk because he cannot find a handle for an ending. He finishes with a lame and mumbled, "Well, I guess that's all I have to say."

An exit line is a crisp statement that can be counted on to get you off the stage or off your feet with no loss of effectiveness. It should be made in a firm voice. An abrupt "Thank you" is neither inspired nor always appropriate. Something like "Thank you for giving me this half hour to tell you how much help disabled workers can be to your company" might be appropriate. Or, "I have enjoyed telling you about management by objectives. I'll be interested in hearing how you make out with it in your company."

"Now, if you have any questions, I will be glad to answer them" is a foolproof ending, if it is applicable.

The important thing is to know when you begin what your exit line is going to be. Memorize it. Then if you have to abridge your talk, you can be sure to finish in a dignified and unflustered manner.

Presentations by Groups Require Special Treatment

A presentation by a group tends to be of special importance or it would not require several persons to make it. It therefore has three or four built-in hazards and requires special planning. Each speaker may consider that what he has to say is the vital part of the proceedings. Each may take too long, and the overall result be a disaster.

In spite of the length, a group presentation may have embarrassing gaps in it, or even contradictions, and not add up to an effective whole. The probable importance of the occasion makes a poor job especially costly.

A planning session with all participants present should decide the strategy to be followed, the controlling purpose, the material to be covered by each speaker, and the order of speakers. It should also decide, if necessary, who is to be in charge, who sums up, who answers questions, and who makes decisions, if any are to be made. Anticipation of key questions and agreement on answers can be the most valuable part of a group planning session.

Rehearsal of a group presentation, with all participants present, is necessary. When the several talks are heard, a certain amount of cutting, adding, and swapping always takes place, to the benefit of the presentation as a whole.

Many group presentations involve enough persons to make initial introductions inadequate. Name tags printed with a felt pen in letters that can be read at least six feet away and announcement of name and function before speaking are both highly desirable. The tags are also useful to identify non-speakers who may accompany speakers. It is often equally useful to have members of a small audience wear tags, too.

When you are host to a group making a presentation, you can contribute to the success of the occasion by insisting on name tags. Since lunch or dinner often precedes a group presentation, place cards, with names written by felt pen on both sides of the cards, will speed better identification.

5

Meeting Different

Types of Situations

The situations in which you will make presentations fall into several types according to purpose. Informational, problem-solving, sales, decision-making, and teaching are the most common. They overlap, of course. They all are informational, they usually involve problems, and usually they are persuasive. But each type tends to have a main purpose of its own and therefore its own dominant characteristics.

Keep Informational Presentations Selective

The chief tests of informational presentations are: Will the audience understand? Will they remember?

The person who gives an informational presentation usually has several handicaps. Because he knows much more about his subject than his audience, he faces a natural temptation to show off his superior knowledge. Therefore he is in danger of underdoing his presentation by taking background material for granted and by using unfamiliar terms without explanation. He is also in danger of overdoing by including an abundance of factual detail and subordinate issues beyond the interest and grasp of the audience.

51

Overdoing is often a manifestation of vanity—the reflection of an unadmitted desire to impress the audience or even hypothetical professional peers who are not present. Or it is evidence of failure, through indifference or misleading instructions, to analyze the audience correctly in advance.

Suppose that you are to give a presentation with slides on the topic "Twentieth Century Wood Engraving," an unlikely but typical informational presentation. Your audience is a woman's club. The members are intelligent, but, naturally enough, totally uninformed about your subject. They almost certainly think you are going to talk about wood carving or etchings. Your audience analysis tells you that in the course of an hour you cannot fill in all the gaps in their knowledge of so specialized a matter. And they are not all that interested anyway. You must simplify—you must select.

So, let us imagine, you decide that in the first five minutes you will show slides that explain what wood engravings are, in the second five minutes you will show sixteenth century woodcuts and nineteenth century wood engravings, and the rest of the time you will concentrate on the work of a half-dozen leading engravers of this century.

What can you expect the club members to understand? To remember? Probably to understand what wood engraving really is—how one is made and what it looks like. More important, to remember with pleasure the character and charm of the best work of this century.

Two or three slides and maybe a demonstration with a wood block and burin can make the essentials of the process clear. Paradoxically, more than five minutes of explanation would plunge the audience into confusing technical matters. Then a solid half hour of slides and perhaps some reproductions, without much attention to the artist or discussion of technique, should build up the pleasurable appreciation of twentieth century wood engravings that is your chief goal.

Simplification of material and emphasis must be carried out by diligent control of text, graphics and other aids. The trick in controlling the text—that is, what you say or write—is selection, stressing, and repetition of key words, phrases, and figures. The brief explanation of any subject revolves around a few key facts and ideas, symbolized by the key words and figures. Select them and make them stand out by the conspicuous place they occupy, by stress from voice, type, or other device, by the lack of competition from similar or subordinate material, and by repetition.

In the wood-engraving presentation, for instance, to make clear what a burin is, you would probably show an enlarged diagram of a burin and a photograph of it being used. For a small audience you might show a real one and use it on a block of wood. You might decide not to use the unusual word burin at all, but just to refer to it as the engraving tool. One unfamiliar term can make a subject seem difficult when it is not.

The effectiveness of selectivity depends on the concentration of the attention of an audience on the essential. Burial of the essential in a welter of less significant information creates blurred impressions and dim memories. Often a digression to explain an incidental point will stick in a listener's mind and lead him to overlook the important ones.

Figures are particularly subject to blurring. It is rarely necessary or desirable to let an audience see all the figures that make up a financial presentation, for instance. Say you are going on TV to explain a bond issue for a new high school. What are the key figures? Number of children of high-school age in the next ten years; number of classrooms needed; cost of a new building now and in the future; and the increase in taxes to pay for the bond issue. These selected figures, translated into appropriate graphics, should be presented boldly by themselves without competition from supporting figures.

Otherwise the way to make sure your presentation does lead to understanding and remembrance is to answer the questions that your audience will want answered. Before a taxpayer can be expected to vote to tax himself further for a new high school, he wants to know: Is a new school really necessary? How much will it cost? How much will my taxes be increased?

In a straight informational presentation, especially one reporting statistical information, you usually have to answer four questions—*why? how? what?* and *so? Why?* requires you to explain the circumstances leading to your report. *How?* requires you to

explain the procedures you followed. *What?* leads to your findings. *So?* requires that you either make recommendations or at
least estimate the significance of your findings. The fourth step,
interpreting your findings, is often the one that merits your most
careful thought.

Problem-Solving Presentations Weigh Alternatives

One suggestion for the designer of a problem-solving presentation is to follow the steps that theoretically underlie the problem-
solving process. Theoretically, because the human mind does not
often function step by step. It may jump to the solution before
a problem is fully stated. It roves about scanning different aspects
of a problem somewhat as a hound runs around picking up a scent.
Yet a presentation gains in effectiveness by taking an audience
through the logical steps, beginning with the true problem and
omitting false moves along the way.

A logical pattern may go something like this:

a) description of the original problem situation
b) statement of the true specific problem finally isolated as
   critical
c) hypotheses about the nature of this critical problem
d) weighing of alternative possible solutions
e) proof of correct solution, or reasons for preferring one
   solution

A prime cause of confusion in problem-solving sessions arises
from the failure of the audience to grasp what the problem really
is. In your presentation, therefore, it is important to state the
problem clearly and simply and then to restate it as you go along.
Use specific words that sum up the problem. Do not use vague
expressions such as, "We cannot let this sort of thing go on."

After you have made what you consider a clear succinct statement of a problem, go over every word and ask yourself: Can
this word be taken in a sense different from the one that I am
using? Can this word be given a wider or narrower meaning than
the one I am employing? In a talk to parents about a college
education for their children, you would do well to stress intel-

lectual development because they tend to rate colleges by the amount of attention the students get. Education may mean something quite different to them from what it means to you.

In a recent meeting leaders of higher education and business discussed for two days the following problem: Business and industry are not attracting the liberal arts college graduate. The discussion resulted in deep confusion. Why? Because the term "liberal arts college graduate" was too inclusive. What the group really wanted to get at was the problem of attracting for future management the intellectual, the student of exceptional conceptualizing ability, with a high concern for human relationships, but no practical skill, as in chemistry. This problem is not the same as what happens to an average liberal arts graduate.

Even the term problem solving itself can be misunderstood. Only in scientific presentations are you likely to deal with correct solutions, and even then you may have a choice. Even in science new solutions supersede old ones that have long been considered the right ones. In the realm of human affairs one solution is not "correct"; it is only more desirable than one or more others. This, then, makes the essence of the presentation a weighing of alternatives. The end of the game is to establish the greater degree of probability of one course of action over one or more others.

To give the audience a clear grasp of the pattern of the presentation, you have to present the alternatives in an unconfusing fashion. You might list them on a chart or slide at once, or you might bring them forth one at a time. You have a choice also whether to disclose your preference at once, at the end of weighing the alternatives, or not at all. Graphics help immensely in clarifying your pattern.

Let us take the problem of the liberal arts graduate. Say that you have to make the final presentation at the meeting cited. You would perhaps first decide that you would make clear what action might be taken, not urge strongly that it be taken. You would then analyze the alternatives as follows: a) The education of the technically oriented undergraduate might include a larger share of humanities and social sciences, even at the expense of delaying some or all of his professional courses until graduate school. b) The non-technical student might be helped to understand the role of business in modern society, and he might be encouraged to study some subjects, such as accounting, of immediate use in business. c) Business might devise programs to attract and hold exceptional liberal arts graduates, whether or not they have immediately useful skills, long enough for them to enter line management.

Without undue emphasis, partly by making it last on your list, you would indicate that the third alternative is the one with the fresh challenge. The first two have to be explored briefly and disposed of. Otherwise someone in the audience will insist on discussing them and thus obscure the vital part of the meeting. The first two alternatives offer partial solutions already in operation with varying degrees of success. The third alternative is really a new solution because it has never been tried in any organized way.

Nothing spectacular about such an analysis—but elegance in any problem-solving presentation consists in analysis so simple that it seems inevitable to the audience.

Sales Presentations Must Persuade

Sales presentations vary in format from the quiet intimacy of a client's or customer's office to a booth in a trade show with crowds shuffling by. TV commercials are sales presentations. They bring in artistic and technical considerations beyond the scope of this book, and they are often objectionable beyond endurance. Yet the TV commercial has one salient characteristic applicable to other presentations. It always has one clear message. "Smoke Faggs and lose weight" may irritate you, but you have no difficulty understanding it. Curiously, the main trouble with many sales presentations is that the central message does not come through clearly and strongly.

The advertising manager of a hospital-supplies firm decides to do an educational film on viruses. He wants it to be educational, not commercial. He hopes that it will combine scientific and artistic excellence. He gets in touch with three film producers, explains his aims, and invites them to visit his company's headquarters and make their presentations.

All three follow exactly the same faulty tactics. They show films that have no scientific elements and only routine photographic interest. They talk for a couple of hours about their organization, equipment, and creative talent. They assert that, though they have no knowledge of viruses, they can pick up enough knowledge in a short time to make a film about any subject... The advertising manager is listening for one message—what they can do to make a scientific film about viruses that will meet his criteria. The film producers do not make a sale because they never send the message he is listening for.

Millions of times each day, in Paris shops, Amsterdam offices, Tokyo teahouses, Cairo bazaars, and Grand Rapids front doors, sales presentations are made. Probably the best are the ones without words, those in the windows of jewelry stores, bake shops, and pet shops, where the objects for sale appeal with their own compelling eloquence. Probably the worst are those made by high-pressure salesmen.

There can be only one aim to a sales presentation—to make a sale, either at once or later on. To accomplish this obvious objective, the sales presentation must persuade.

Persuasion acts on two levels—the logical and the emotional. The emotional enters into sales presentations far more than most salesmen seem to realize. Whether in Bombay or Brooklyn, the sale is already lost if the buyer thinks he must obey the motto "Caveat emptor." The sale is half made if the buyer feels he can trust the seller, not beware of him. If the salesman is frenetic, indifferent, or bumbling, the buyer feels repelled. Poise, definiteness, and controlled enthusiasm evoke trust.

Yet if a person enters into a selling situation at all, to some degree he unconsciously wants to buy. Buying things is comforting, reassuring, ego-building. But the sensible, censorious self within the buyer is on guard, like a watchdog, to kill the fun. Whether the dog barks or wags his tail is up to the seller.

A man stops at the tie counter in a men's shop. He could use a new tie, he thinks, one or perhaps two, of those dark silks. Most of those he has have lost their freshness. He is tired of them. And most of them his wife and daughters picked out anyway. At this point, the watchdog stands up and looks stern. If the salesman behind the counter looks supercilious, the customer eyes the $6.50 price tag and virtuously passes on. But if the salesman smiles and says, as though to a fellow connoisseur, "Unusual English Maccles-fields, don't you think, sir?" and makes a deft knot on one hand, the dog wags his tail. Our hero stands still. He no longer sees ties; he is looking at rich remarkable English Macclesfields. His excru-ciating decision is whether or not he can limit himself to two.

Enthusiasm about the merits of a product or a service and con-viction about its value to the customer are fundamental to a sales presentation. The emotional reactions of the customer are often heightened by sensory impressions. For example, the rich look of the silk neckties and the impression made by the one that the salesman knots on his fingers create pleasurable sensations.

But a sales situation that involves a presentation in the sense that we are generally using the term must also appeal to the rea-son of the audience. That means that it must answer all the ques-tions that the audience may logically ask. Even in the simple necktie example, how many salesmen would be able to give a convincing answer if the customer asked—What is the difference in quality between these ties at $6.50 and those over there at $3.95?

In any sales presentation your essential responsibility is to make crystal clear to the audience the benefits that will accrue to him if he buys whatever you are selling. Merely praising its virtues is not enough. He does not want to know that a necktie, for instance, is "of the finest quality that money can buy." He wants to know that, because it is made of the finest natural silk threads, it will tie 500 times without wrinkling or showing wear, or something equally factual. Unless your presentation includes believable evi-dence of the superiority of your product or service over others that are available, your audience will often silently decide in favor of your competition.

The success of a sales presentation, therefore, from start to finish depends on its persuasiveness. Persuasion is a mixture of appeals to the head and appeals to the emotions, with the propor-tions adjusted to the taste of particular audiences.

In any persuasive presentation you must have a clear idea of what objections you are likely to meet, what compromises you may be willing to make, and what terms both sides may conceivably settle on. To be this flexible, you often have to secure approval from your superiors in advance. Failure to do so may mean that you waste time checking back or make commitments without authority—commitments that therefore may not be honored or may get you in hot water.

Persuasion often depends on defining the area of common interest between you and your audience. When a builder says, "I want you to be completely satisfied with your house, Mrs. Lang, because if you are, you can help me sell more houses in Sheraton Acres," he is defining the intersection of lines of interest. Mrs. Lang believes that the builder is treating her well because it is to his advantage to do so. An appeal to taxpayers to support a bond issue for a new high school would stress the obvious common denominator of children for parents with children of high school age and for other taxpayers the need for better educational facilities to attract new industry and employees.

In a complex situation—say, negotiating a sales distributorship—getting ready might involve what in diplomatic circles is called a "position paper." This is simply a writing down of the main arguments pro and con and matching up possible moves by both sides: "If they ask for an exclusive distributorship, we'll offer them the Eastern seaboard and no more. If they won't accept that, we'll offer them everything west of the Mississippi. That's it."

Presentations for Decision-Makers Must Be Complete

Presentations are a common prelude to decision-making. They analyze a recommended course of action—why action is necessary, the alternatives, exposition of the action recommended, the feasibility of the action, and the benefits from it. Such presentations range from being as objective and factual as possible to being openly persuasive. Another type merely analyzes the various alternatives and leaves the choice to the decision-makers.

Presentations for executives who are making decisions have one characteristic in common, one not necessarily present in other types—they must be complete. This often means including an analysis of the background of the subject—the total problem. Say that you make a presentation to a management group on the benefits of a new company hospital-insurance plan, for instance. It would sound fatuous to them if it showed no awareness of the past experience of the company with other plans and the impact of the new plan on relations with the union.

Let us see how executive decision-making proceeds in a typical corporation.

The management group of an Oregon food-processing company think that perhaps they should have a second plant to serve their customers in the East more efficiently. The director of planning makes a preliminary economic study of the proposal and then presents his findings to the president and other key management men. They accept his evidence that a second plant in the East would be desirable.

The president then asks the vice president for engineering to conduct a search for a plant site and prepare an estimate of the cost of it and a new plant. When the search is completed, the vice president for engineering presents the advantages and disadvantages of four sites in New England. One in Connecticut is chosen.

Then at the next meeting of the board of directors the president presents the economic justification for a new plant, and the vice president for engineering presents the reasons for choosing the plant site in Connecticut. The board approves an authorization of $10 million to go ahead with the project.

In essence, this fictitious example stands for a scene, often a dramatic one, enacted daily. Someone in the management group of a company, a city, a university, or other large organization points to a critical problem or suggests a major action. The problem or suggestion is researched by someone else—often by several persons in different departments. Progress reports of findings are often given at several management levels during the course of months. The final decision may commit the organization to an action involving millions of dollars, changing the character of the organization, and affecting the careers of many employees.

Obvious, but not generally noted, is the importance of presentations in this pattern of decision-making. Along the way a number of executives—it may be several; it may be dozens—including the president or other chief executive officer and governing board, make up their minds on the basis of their experience and the presentations they hear and read. The person who controls the preparation of a presentation, therefore, to a degree controls the decision. How constructive his influence is, depends first of all on his ability to gather information and reason about the issues involved. Then it depends on his skill in preparing the presentation so that the audience receives the message objectively, yet in a clear and interesting fashion.

Training Presentations Must Teach

Every executive is a teacher. Every teacher gives presentations. The difference is that the executive is usually engaged in training; the teacher in education. Sometimes the difference seems as Demosthenes put it long ago: "You make them say, 'How well he speaks.' I make them say, 'Let us march against Philip.'"

In its simpler forms training means teaching someone how to do something. No one learns how to do except by doing. No one learns how to do anything much by listening to speeches. Your first question in preparing an ordinary training presentation, therefore, is—what sort of audio-visual aids will best convey a tactile sense of the process being taught?

Training in repairing machines might start with diagrammatic charts or models that explain the construction and operation in simplified terms. Then the repair procedure, broken down into simplified steps, might be represented by a filmstrip of stop-action stills. The last two steps in the presentation might be a) a demonstration on a machine by the instructor and b) a now-you-do-it, one step at a time, by members of the training group.

The training presentations made by executives tend to be more complex, less tactile than the kind that takes place in shop courses. Demonstrating to automobile dealers the features of a new-model car, briefing field agents of a government department on a major change in legislation, and showing a group of plant managers how to use data processing in inventory control are more typical situations facing executives. Yet they all aim to teach. And in the world of automobile dealers, government agents, and industrial plant managers, as in the shop, the efficacy of the teaching is measurable. The burden is on the presenter. He does not hand out grades to his audience. He receives grades according to whether or not they understand and "march against Philip."

Suppose we look at these three representative training situations and imagine the form such teaching might take outside of classrooms. A new model car might be literally unveiled at a dinner of automobile dealers. A company officer might then discuss its virtues as it revolves on a turntable on a platform in a hotel ballroom. There might be a motion picture to demonstrate the car's road performance and a filmstrip to point up specific improvements in styling and engine design. Then also by filmstrip might be shown the advertising and sales promotion plans, including appearances by stars of TV shows on which the car is to be advertised. Perhaps last would be a pep talk on pricing and sales. The major purpose of the evening would be to make the changes clear, to build up in the minds of the dealers the conviction that the car is the best of its class, and to arouse enough enthusiasm about selling it so that they would place orders in the optimistic amounts hoped for by the car manufacturer.

A group of field representatives of a government agency would receive less glamorous training. They would be called in for a day or so. First, they probably would be given a general talk by the head of the department about the aim and main features of the program. Then, they would review the legislation item by item together with printed material for them to distribute. Typical cases might be highlighted by charts or slides. Then perhaps the session would end with role playing to give each agent a chance to prove his grasp of the details of the new program. Apart from a belief in the beneficial nature of the legislation, precise understanding of its workings would be the aim of this training session.

The presentation of a new inventory control system to a group of plant managers would aim at general understanding and acceptance. The effort would be to train them in how to make use of the system, not how to run it. The plant managers would mainly need to be taught how new electronic communication devices can scan inventories of goods at different warehouses and feed back to plants data on which to base production schedules.

A chart showing in stylized form the flow of information, the time lapse for each step, the type of information transmitted, and the role of different groups would be the key to this presentation. The chart could be formed from several large pieces of illustration board ranged across the front of a room. Or multiple images on a three-module screen would be more effective in showing the movement of information through the phases of the process.

This is the kind of teaching where the audience must visualize what takes place. The plant managers do not need to know, at this time, the technicalities. They need to learn the essential facts of what information can be made available to them and how fast. This knowledge should convince them of the efficiency and savings to be gained through scientific inventory control. It should make them eager to cooperate in adopting the system. They would then willingly designate staff men to take an extended course in data processing in order to work on the team with marketing services and management information men.

Most teachers, especially those in colleges and universities, have never thought of themselves as engaged in making presentations. Yet they are. They are trying not merely to explain subject matter, but to arouse interest, establish significance, and motivate to action —to further study and often to lifetime commitment.

Yet outside of science, where demonstrations and laboratory experiments break the dreariness of lectures, the chief means of teaching is still the spoken word, as it has been for centuries. Suppose educators were to apply the same simple test of the effectiveness of their teaching that businessmen, athletic coaches, and public officials apply to their presentations—that their listeners understand the message, be convinced of its significance, and take the action recommended. Classroom presentations would certainly take on an aspect of professional competence which is now lacking.

It is true that educational films are adding lustre to classrooms across the nation. The Hall of Science at the University of California, for instance, produces films that employ resources of scientists and equipment beyond the command of any single teacher. They supplement regular course work with splendid photography and precise explanation. National Educational Television makes available a bounteous store of filmed material that richly supplements the study of the sciences, social sciences, and humanities. What can a professor say about a Greek play that communicates to a student anything as vital as a filmed performance of the play itself?

The handwriting is on the blackboard. The rising tide of students is forcing schools and colleges to take more interest in the learning process. Closed-circuit television, language recordings, teaching machines, and other audio-visual aids are joining motion pictures as substitutes for listening to teachers talk. Having by necessity to work independently, the student is becoming more curious, self-reliant, and creative. Constantly squeezed by higher costs, industry improves its processes and products. Education will do the same.

Part II

Graphics and Other

Audio-Visual Aids

6

The Role of

Audio-Visual Aids

Audio-Visual Aids Are Basic to Presentations

Graphics and other audio-visual aids are in common use wherever presentations are habitually given. Presentations and graphics both derive their reason for being from the same source—the prevalence of statistical and technical data in decision-influencing communication. Such data have minor significance in the lives of musicians, housekeepers, English teachers, and others who rarely use the word presentation. In science, government, industry, and business, statistics and technical information have a major role, and their communication requires visualization to aid the audience to grasp them.

Often the essence of your presentation will appear in the graphics. Your central ideas and most important facts will be boiled down to what is on your charts or slides. Then your voice or written commentary amplifies, interprets, and stresses what the audience sees, but it introduces no new basic material. At other times the graphics add clarity to the text or are only incidental. In both cases creative use of audio-visual aids can make the difference between a well-accepted presentation and one that does not

get across. Colorful charts, cheerful music, and humorous drawings can save a training film, for instance, from being deadly.

Visual aids can help you, as well as the audience. They can
guarantee that you will remember your main points and their
order. And they can give the audience a sense of sharing as your
thoughts unfold.

Imagine that you are a development engineer making a presentation to a new product committee about product PA800, a new
paper adhesive. The clumsy way is to write out everything you
want to say and then half read, half talk your way through. Or
you can shuffle through a stack of notes. Or you can put your
material on charts under the following headings: 1) the paper
adhesive market, 2) competitive products, and 3) adhesive PA800.

You put down under 1) the most important uses of adhesives
for paper and the estimated sales, under 2) the share of the market enjoyed by the leading products, their prices, and their virtues
and faults, and then under 3) comparative information about
product PA800. You write additional facts and cues lightly in
pencil on your charts. From a short distance such lightly pencilled
notes are not noticeable.

You are now in no danger whatever of forgetting your piece.
It is set forth boldly before you. You and your audience can see
at a glance the schema for what you are saying. You and your
audience are never in doubt about what comes next or about
which items are main and which subordinate. Your charts keep
you on the beam, and your audience, too.

Graphics and Other Aids Must Be Justified

The first question to ask yourself before deciding on using
graphics or other aids to a presentation is—should I? Probably as
many talks have been ruined by audio-visual aids as have been
helped by them. A lack of aids is a known hazard. To use charts,
films, or other aids involves putting your foot in a potential booby
trap.

The basic danger of all audio-visual aids is that they do attract
attention—by definition. Therefore, they introduce a divisive element, in the oral presentation, at least. The attention of the lis-

teners is divided between the spoken word and whatever else they hear and see. An audience may rate highly a presentation that employs aids in clever ways. But listeners may judge presentations by their entertaniment value, not by their true effectiveness. The only presentation rating that you should take seriously is the degree of success you have in achieving your purpose.

These reservations suggest that at the outset of a talk you should weigh carefully whether or not to use graphics or other aids. Then, if so, what aids should you use and to what degree?

You should use mechanical aids only when you are certain that you can enhance your presentation sufficiently to justify the trouble—and often the expense—and the risk of distracting the audience. Justification begins when you can make significant aspects of your message more memorable by the use of charts, films, music, or other sensory effects beyond your unassisted voice.

You know you can use graphics profitably when you wish to talk about such matters as budgets or chemical formulas that cannot easily be grasped or cannot be carried in mind merely by being heard. In certain circumstances, images, as in films or tangible objects (as in demonstrations), may be more effective than abstract figures and graphs.

Understand the Contribution
Audio-Visual Aids Can Make

Audio-visual aids can be used only when you have the technical skill or assistance to prepare and handle them properly. Have you ever tried to use an unfamiliar tape recorder and found yourself keeping a roomful of people waiting while you re-invented the thing?

You use audio-visual aids when you have the time to choose the right ones, prepare them properly, and rehearse your presentation with them. Finding the right aids and using them in the right way cannot be improvised and cannot be done properly at the last minute.

The audio-visual aids discussed here are available to you in most organizations, or should be. Your personnel department, public relations department, or advertising agency can advise you about them. Most large companies, universities, and government agencies have special audio-visual aid departments. Staff members prepare graphics and other aids and often handle them during presentations. But it is desirable that you be familiar with all the forms, so that you can decide when to use them and prepare your material properly for them. Devices are constantly being improved, but you cannot count on having access to new models.

The major forms of audio-visual aids that you are likely to use are:

Graphics—words, figures, tables, graphs, drawings, photographs, etc., presented on easel charts, blackboards, stick-on boards, and similar flat surfaces

Projection—slides, motion picture films, filmstrips, and overhead projectors

Sound—public address systems, sound film, tape recorders, records, and music

Demonstrations—sample products, models, role playing

Exhibits—sample products, charts, photographs, models, and projection

Written material—typed and printed

The American Management Association, Eastman Kodak, and other organizations have workshops on the preparation and use of graphics and other presentation aids. If you are involved seriously in presentations, you should attend such a workshop. Eastman Kodak, 3M, and other companies that manufacture audio-visual materials and equipment will send you useful printed matter on request.

Graphics have two prime functions—first, to simplify facts, figures, and ideas (especially when they are complex) and second, to help make the logic of the conclusions reached seem clear and inevitable. To carry out these two functions, graphics often are representations of *quantities* of money, weight, time, objects, people, and so on. Ideas may be represented by key words, and they may also be symbolically represented by pictures.

To encourage voters to be well informed, a poster (which is a form of presentation) in a community center carries the slogan, "It is your privilege to vote; it is your duty to be well informed." In addition it shows a cartoon of a voter approaching a voting booth carrying an armload of books, dragging a TV set, and listening to a transistor radio. Pictures can convey some information literally—a photograph of an accident in a court case, a film about a school for the deaf, and so on.

Good graphics do more than eliminate non-essentials; they also point out unmistakably what line of reasoning to follow. One normal pattern is that of a trend. Sometimes something as obvious as an arrow can show the direction of change. Often comparison is the pattern. Then contrasting colors can help. A photograph of an accident can help determine the cause and responsibility, for instance; a film about a school for deaf children can move the public to contribute to its support.

One widely recommended rule is never to put on a chart or slide more than the audience can comprehend in thirty seconds. The only way that this can be accomplished is to limit yourself to one clear point and to put down nothing that you do not mention. For most presentations this rigorous selection will do wonders. In presentations of familiar material a professional audience can grasp rapidly a good deal of detail, as long as it is accurate, organized, and clearly visible. But the amount of detail is less than most technical speakers care to admit. They fail to make allowance for the difference between graphics in a report, article, or book to be consulted at leisure and graphics for a one- or two-minute exposure.

The Use of Graphics Calls for Sound Judgment

A detached analysis of your material is your first step toward simplification. What are the essential points that *must* be communicated? Can the number of these points be cut down? Can the figures be rounded off? Will one or two words do for captions in place of five or six? Can some of the figures in a series be skipped, as some clocks have only quarter-hour figures?

But the important decision is to omit actual material. This means suppressing secondary material. It may have significance, or it may be interesting; but it is not primary. So you leave it out entirely. Or perhaps you hold it in reserve for mention, if time permits, perhaps during the question period. In either case you cut it from your graphics.

A more sophisticated action is to *translate* the complex material of original copy into simplified graphic terms. The most pertinent example is that of the translation of tables of figures into graphs. Often, however, the original graphs are only way-stages on the road to a final synthesis of greater clarity and elegance. All scientific thinking has this end in view—to state the complex and difficult in such a way that it cannot be further simplified and thus achieves a certain esthetic quality, or elegance.

A fundamental question to ask yourself is, What is the precise relationship between my graphics and my talk or words? Are my graphics mere adjuncts to my written or spoken explanation? Or are graphics—at least in reference to a specific piece of material— my chief form of communication, with words largely background or clarifications of the diagram, graph, or other image? If you elect to use graphics, you may be surprised at how often you will have a more effective presentation if your graphics come close to telling their own story.

In a well-conceived chart you can see how the use of key words only, plus the conception of the design, enables you to imagine the structure of the entire talk without hearing it.

Graphics should be planned to give a unified effect. Lack of such planning results in different types of lettering, numerical scales, and artistic styles. Then the effect is one of disconnected parts.

Therefore, it is desirable to get together early in the planning stage with whoever in your organization may guide you. While the director of presentations advocated in Chapter 1 probably has no counterpart in your organization, you would do well to invest someone with a similar role in relation to your presentation. He may be your boss, your assistant, a sales training manager, or any person with appropriate experience.

In addition, if at all possible, you should bring in someone who really knows the technicalities of audio-visual aids. You may turn to two or three persons—a graphics man, a photographer, and, if he is available, a designer. A designer may be found in an advertising department or agency, at a good printing plant, or in a packaging department. In companies where desgin is an important element of the business, an entire design department rich with talent may be at your disposal. There is almost always more help available to persons making presentations than they have the wit to use.

From an early conference on the strategy of your presentation and the techniques to be used should come a decision, let us say to use slides. Your preliminary analysis should indicate how many. Your advisers can then tell you, if you do not know, when your final copy has to be ready, what sort of intermediate graphic treatment should be given to it, and when finished slides will be ready. You will then know how much time you will have to rehearse with your slides.

Against a background of such planning, you soon find yourself faced with the pleasant realization that the essentials of your presentation are right there before you in a handful of slides or the corresponding copy. If then you work from these essentials, you may discover to your delight that, *in terms of material,* your presentation is completed in the rough. This discovery may be thrust on you by your time limit. Merely sketching in what you intend to say in an unpolished review with your advisers may take you an hour when you have only half an hour for your presentation. By putting your graphics together first, you save yourself from spending twice as much time writing out a presentation and then abstracting the copy for graphics afterwards.

An early conference that includes consideration of audio-visual elements may lead to much more fundamental decisions. In a certain situation, for instance, what started out as a single presentation may turn into a series for many audiences. Or it may seem desirable to make the same material into a film clip for distribution to commercial television stations. For this shorter version a well known announcer or actor might read the script. Such decisions can change the character of a presentation and make a different approach to the audio-visuals necessary.

In ordinary circumstances deciding on what the audio-visual material will be and what technique will be most effective in the specific situation has two valuable results: It shakes down the presentation to essentials; and it ensures having the graphics or other aids ready in time for adequate rehearsing.

You Need the Services of an Audio-Visual Department

Since making presentations is a part of the daily routine of most organizations of any size, audio-visual departments are fairly common. They are by no means universal, though they are as necessary to supply services to persons making presentations as secretaries are to persons handling correspondence. In general existing departments tend to have staffs who are overwhelmed trying to keep up with routine lettering and photographic jobs. They are usually short on management with broad professional experience.

Ideally, the head of an audio-visual department should be someone who has much the same breadth as our imaginary director of presentations *plus* professional familiarity with all the audio-visual techniques. Realistically, he ought to start at least with a background of experience in some field such as industrial design or film making, not just be a person skilled in audio-visual mechanics or in the managing of unrelated activities.

The head of an audio-visual department should be able to advise from the beginning about the two major audio-visual aspects of a presentation—effectiveness of communication and mechanics. He should be able to say to someone: "I think you would be better off using three cardboard charts than with all these slides"; or "We could do a safety film ourselves, using the men in the plant"; or "There's a studio in Chicago that can take your script and turn it into a first-rate filmstrip with cartoons, narration, and music for about $4500."

A minimum staff consists of a photographer, a freehand chart letterer, and a graph maker, especially for slides and written presentations. As in every other kind of work, the person who has to be told precisely what to do is often a liability; the person who can do more than his job calls for is priceless. You will be lucky to find an audio-visual person who tries to understand the communication problem posed by the physical setting of a specific presentation—or who understands why one style of type is suitable for certain subject matter and not at all for something else— or who has rational standards for judging the effectiveness of a film.

If your organization does not have a fully rounded audio-visual department, for an important presentation you should consider hiring an audio-visual firm to help you. An advertising agency or a public relations firm may or may not be competent to give you the help you need.

Since a great deal of the material shown at presentations is confidential, precautions must be taken to safeguard its security. Members of an audio-visual department must be carefully chosen for their trustworthiness. The area where they work should be inaccessible to others. Their discussions about work to be done should take place in a separate area. They should be trained to know who may see what material and to apply the "need-to-know" rule to anything else.

At the same time, all persons in an organization who deal with an audio-visual department must be trained to observe similar care. Confidential material should never be sent to outside agencies without the approval of the proper authorities. Someone should check periodically to see how well security is being observed in the handling of audio-visual material. Much too often the laxness is hair-raising.

A word of warning about the technical complexity of audio-visual aids comes here. The mechanisms available and their accessories and the companies manufacturing them, distributing them, and providing services that go with them are bewildering to the layman and often to persons who have more than casual proficiency in their use. In your public library are books and magazines that can give you an introduction to the various forms. Even browsing through a publication like "Film and Audio-Visual Annual" should convince you that you will do well to leave the mysteries of the multitudinous mechanisms to the experts while you concentrate on learning how to use them to strengthen your presentations.

Rooms Should Be Designed for Presentations

The head of a New York advertising agency was recently asked to present to the board of directors of a corporation the capabilities of his agency to handle the advertising of the corporation. His staff worked overtime for several weeks and finally put together a filmstrip that they believed to be irresistible. On the appointed day the advertising executive waited in the handsome reception room of the company's headquarters in a tall new glass-sided building in mid-Manhattan. Then on the minute, carrying his projector and folding screen, he was ushered into the board room. After a hurried introduction, he set up his equipment and then had to crawl around the floor to find a plug and to drag his cord under the table among the legs of the directors. Shaken, he *then* found to his incredulous dismay that there were no drapes on the twenty-foot window that stretched along the entire side of the board room. Demoralized, he ran through his presentation with the images on his filmstrip pale and wan in the glare of sunlight from the window.

The best aid any presentation can have is the right room. The way to ensure this happy state is to determine generously what presentation needs exist before a building is built and then to agree with the architect on locations. Thereafter the architect, an audio-visual engineer, and the equivalent of a director of presentations for the organization should work together to design the facilities properly. More thought and expense go into the designing of reception rooms than usually go into designing rooms for presentation purposes. In fact, a room completely designed for presentations is rare.

Obviously enough, no single room can meet all situations. What, then, are the normal needs? The two basic needs for presentation rooms of all sorts are a desirable environment and good audio-visual facilities.

A satisfactory environment for a presentation is one that harmonizes with and, if possible, promotes its purpose. Thus, if a salesman is able to get into the crowded office of the design engineer who will write the specifications that affect his product, he is happy. He would rather make his presentation there than in a well equipped conference room to people who have no voice in the decision. Internal presentations by members of an organization may get a better hearing from colleagues if they are given in the president's office or the board room—the environment suggests importance and even sanction.

Otherwise, what aspects of the environment should be considered in setting up rooms specifically designed for presentations? Convenience is a main factor. An ideally equipped presentation room will be used spottily if it is out of the way. It can be out of the way psychologically as well as physically. It might be too close to "officers' country" or too public, if it has windows on a hall. Lack of security may limit the usefulness of one room, crowdedness another, bleakness of atmosphere another, and so on. Habitual noise outside a room, near the kitchen of a dining room, for instance, should bar its use for presentations. But access to coffee is desirable. Quiet air conditioning is a must. Nothing you or your audio-visual aids can do will offset the effect on an audience of a room that is hot and oxygen-less.

Proper environment, therefore, should be determined by conditions of use. Who normally use a room for presentations and under what prevailing circumstances? The same conditions determine the appointments and audio-visual equipment. One room for high-level transactions might have concealed equipment behind panelled walls with push-button operation; another for training new salesmen might have display cabinets for products. Round tables and hollow-square arrangements are conducive to small group participation. Theater and schoolroom arrangements are necessary for formal and film presentations to larger groups.

Except for such adjustments to special purposes, a good presentation room needs to provide the following: First, it should be larger than needed for its usual purpose, so that a 25%–50% increase in attendance will not create a disturbance. For a board room set-up about 20 square feet per person is adequate; for a hollow-square table set-up, about 30 feet. Chairs should be comfortable and have arm rests, but they should not be conducive to slumber. They should be satisfactory for writing, either at a table or with a drop tablet arm. They should stack, and extra chairs should be stored near at hand.

Presentation rooms should be windowless. Pulling shades down and up causes an unseemly commotion and never keeps all the light out. A rheostat for controlling all lights in the room should be at the speaker's lectern or within reaching distance. If that is not possible, they should be able to be controlled by one other person.

Standard audio-visual aids should be readily at hand in a room designated for presentations. Ideally, they should be as much a part of the room design as possible, and should be controllable from the speaker's lectern. As a compromise, movable equipment ought to be kept in an adjacent room with technicians in charge, not a quarter of a mile away. Hasty decisions about what kinds of equipment members of an organization *should* use cause difficulties later. Plans should take into account the needs and problems of all the normal aids—lectern, public address system, charts, and projection. A glassed-in control room between two presentation rooms, with slide and motion picture projectors set up to serve both is highly desirable.

An industrial designer or architect can do a great deal to get rid of the clutter and make a room attractive. For instance, roll-back panelling can give a room a lift and serve to conceal a blackboard and projection screen when they are not in use. A board room, used also for regular executive management meetings and occasionally for intimate executive meetings, can be designed to be an executive information center as well as a meeting and presentation room. In a floor-to-ceiling compartment at one end of the room cabinets can be built for financial and other records. Newly-designed top-management meeting rooms should be tied in with computerized management information centers. Soon current data can be flashed on closed-circuit TV monitors.

Few organizations need a large auditorium for presentations. Most sizable organizations can use an auditorium type of room seating 200–300 people. Such a room has either a platform for speakers or inclined seating, or both. Nothing is worse than a presentation to an audience of any size—anything over 50—in a large low-ceilinged room with neither platform nor rising seats. At any rate, the first criterion of ideality is that speakers, charts, and screen must be clearly visible from every seat. If a large room must be used for other purposes that require a flat floor, then a platform is necessary, though it does not assure visibility. A high screen will tire persons in the front seats if they have to tilt their heads back to see. Multipurpose rooms have a way of being ideal for no purpose.

Much better is the inclined floor with the seats rising in a fan. A flat area at the base of the fan, instead of a platform, offers space for chairs and tables for smaller groups. The floor then can rise so that the screen and the speaker's lectern approach the eye-level of the audience. Ideally, the screen should be three modules wide for multiple images from two or even three projectors. Then slides can be made to fade from one to another without awkward blank glare.

In any large room excellent acoustics should be a goal of expert engineering. It is possible, as in the Strosacker Auditorium at Case Institute of Technology, to design an auditorium where a normal speaking voice can be clearly heard from every seat in the room. Nevertheless, while every effort should be made to attain this happy acoustical state, it is well to put in wiring for a public address system—and then to use it.

7

Upgrading Your

Charts

Of all forms of graphics, the chart is the most universal because it is the simplest to use, most readily available, and most flexible. A chart has a primary meaning of being words or tables displayed on a sheet of paper. Somewhat more broadly, all sheets used for presentation purposes are referred to as charts, no matter what symbols or images are placed on them or how arranged. A chart may hold an entire sentence, a graph, a diagram, or a drawing, for instance. By extension, words, graphs, tables and other presentation material placed on a slide or film are referred to as charts. In all uses of the word there lurks a dim awareness of the original prototype of words and tables on paper.

The fact that charts are used in millions of presentations does not mean that they get better and better. Too often they reflect a lack of sophistication extending to sheer indifference and ineptness.

The personnel director of a large corporation recently appeared on the program of a meeting of a national business organization. His dozen charts were grimy and crowded. They clearly had been used for several years for conference-room presentations to small groups in the many plants and offices of his corporation. They contained much detail applicable only to employees of his corporation, and they were unreadable beyond the first few rows of the hotel ballroom where the meeting was held. Because of the irritating impression made by the charts, the audience of 700 discounted the speaker's message and felt that he was a poor representative of his highly respected company.

With inconsequential expense, reasonable attention, and a certain degree of sophistication, you can upgrade your charts. You can change them from stodgy or annoying adjuncts of a presentation to attractive additions. You can make an audience pay close attention, follow the argument more readily, and even relish the occasion a little more. By using first-rate charts, you unobtrusively pay the audience a compliment that they cannot fail to appreciate. You also are showing self-respect. No professional golfer uses mail-order clubs.

Choose the Right Materials

For different occasions you use paper of different quality. For the most informal "inside" occasion such as a first tentative rehearsal, you might use cheap newsprint. Next come varying grades of white paper. Then there are different weights of card, the best being illustration board.

In any organization where presentations are common, it pays to use for all ordinary purposes a good grade of white paper that does not tear easily. When bought in quantity, this stock should have half-inch grids printed on the sheets in pale blue ink. These lines then can be used as guides in lettering and in drawing graphs. It takes an inordinate amount of time for an amateur to lay out guide lines on a large piece of plain chart paper. The half-inch grid makes all measurements quick and accurate and all ratios easy to calculate. The grid is inconspicuous from a few feet; further away it is not noticed at all.

Sometimes for a formal presentation you will use thin card or illustration board. This choice is desirable when a chart is more or less permanent—when it is to be used many times and must be kept fresh looking. It is also desirable when you are paying for professional lettering and design.

Card offers a larger working surface than limp paper does. Paper more than 30 inches wide is hard to handle. Since heavy card can be stood up as well as hung up, it is suitable for use with a table easel for small group presentations. Card is more expensive than paper and heavier to carry on trips, though thin card is often a satisfactory compromise. With good art work, card adds a professional touch to a presentation that paper cannot match.

Chart paper often comes in large pads. Sheets can therefore be torn off as a presentation proceeds—an inept, messy, and distracting action and one that often destroys useful and expensive charts. Or the sheets can be flipped over, thus the term flip-charts. This action too can be distracting unless done smoothly.

You may find chart paper with holes at the top more useful. You can hang it on pegs on easels or walls. If you are in charge of the situation or can persuade someone to do so, have four sets of pegs available. Then you can hang two sets of charts side by side, often a necessary device to show inescapably wide detail as in a table of organization or a PERT or other flow diagram. You can also hang on one side a summary chart, to which the audience can refer as you take up the main points in sequence. On the lower set of pegs you can hang the sheets as you finish with them. By turning them face down as you proceed, you will have them neatly in order when you finish. If you are standing on a platform or if the audience is small enough, sometimes you will have reason to put charts face out on the lower pegs also.

Easels range from heavy wooden affairs that are hard to move to folding aluminum ones that tend to topple over. You have to watch out not to trip over the extended feet of easels. A recent desirable innovation is a double-faced, A-shaped easel that swivels around easily. It has a single upright support with rollers on the base.

Aluminum easels have the virtue of being portable, and there are table-top arrangements of various kinds for small group presentations. Or you can easily make your own. Be certain that an easel suitable for your sheets of paper or card charts is available wherever you are going to give a presentation. Otherwise take your own along. You may find that the pegs in one easel are set apart at a width different from that of your paper. Or you may find that an easel has no pegs; it holds sheets by means of a spring clamp. If you have a lot of charts and especially if they are on card, the clamp may not hold all of your charts at once.

Follow These Suggestions for Laying Out Copy

Lay out your chart first on a scratch pad, or, better, on ordinary graph paper. Observe the same proportions that you will want on your chart. Thus you can design your arrangement and edit your copy, to be sure you have the correct spelling of words, the correct figures or symbols, and the most effective wording.

To lay out copy or graphs in the proper proportion for a chart— or much more important, for a slide—follow this procedure: First, on a sheet of the chart paper to be used (or a piece of newspaper the same size) lay out a rectangle enclosing what will be the actual working area within generous margins, double at the bottom. Draw a diagonal from lower left to upper right. Place your copy paper or graph paper on top so that the lower left corner coincides with that of the working area of the chart paper. Any rectangle on the copy or graph sheet erected on the diagonal is in proportion to the working area of the chart paper.

If, as is almost always the rule, the copy is prepared first with no thought of the shape of the chart paper, the working area on the chart paper can be determined by reversing the procedure. In this case the left corner of the working area of the copy or graph sheet (again, you must allow for margins) is imposed on the left corner of the working area of the chart paper. Then any rectangle erected on the extended diagonal of the copy or graph sheet is in proportion to the copy or graph sheet. But since the shape of this rectangle may be significantly different from that of the chart paper, you will have to adjust the margins.

You can see that the second procedure is less exact than the first and may lead to acute embarrassment. This embarrassment is common in the preparation of copy for slides because slides are projected with the long dimension at the top. Copy prepared with the long dimension on the side then has to be squeezed down and leaves awkward wide areas of empty space on the sides.

Experienced graphics artists, of course, try to make copy fit pleasingly on chart paper or slide no matter how the copy given them looks. But whether you make your own final charts or have someone else (who often is not ingenious about rearranging your proportions) do it, the intelligent way to make sure the proportions of your copy are right is to follow the recommended first procedure. This is no hardship. Once you have established the proper proportions of copy sheets to charts *and* slides, you can automatically lay out your copy within the right dimensions ever after. If you lay out charts frequently, you can save time by making plastic or cardboard templates of the sizes you use most.

The greatest single mistake made in presentations is too much copy on a single chart. Over and over again, this error of judgment ruins what otherwise might be good presentations. Usually the cluttered chart results from the inclusion of so much detail in the presentation that either the main points are obscured or the presentation lasts too long.

You face two fundamentally different presentation situations. One is a presentation of the merits-of-a-product type where the charts exist only to reinforce a few key facts or ideas. The other, such as an explanatory technical talk, may require a good deal more graphic detail. A diagram of a chemical process or a report of a city manager on an annual budget obviously can stand only so much simplification. Nevertheless, you are defeating your own ends if you crowd your chart with so much copy that either the audience cannot read it or they are confused by it.

The ideal charts are those that are uncluttered and highly legible. No more than one, two, maybe three words to a line is a good rule. Once more, plan your chart on a pad first. Make several rough drafts. Do not try to make the first one perfect, especially by erasing.

If you are having your graphics done by someone else, have an editor or other competent adviser check your copy before you give it to an artist. You cannot expect even a professional to put a lot of copy on one sheet without crowding. Nor can you expect him to spell for you, unscramble abbreviations, or undo errors of fact. Give your artist exactly the copy as you want it to be. Give him *clear, legible, accurate, final* copy.

Failure to proofread carefully can be embarrassing when someone in the audience points out an error in arithmetic or the whole audience laughs at a comic misspelling. Errors in your graphics can discredit your entire presentation.

A graphic outline of your subject should be done visually and not in the manner of a freshman theme. Avoid meaningless A's and B's and sub-numerals. Unless you must refer to items by numbers, as, "the seventh step in the process," it is well to omit all outline numbers and letters. They often lead to confusion because they seem part of the text.

Stressing major steps is desirable. If you believe several numbers or letters are necessary, keep them away from the rest of the copy. Symbols, such as circles, squares, and dots, can be used effectively to indicate major items.

If you are forced to put a good deal of copy on a chart, the best you can do to avoid the sense of crowding is to pull the subheads together but space generously between units.

Printers, painters, and graphics designers all design with "air" —that is, with the space around their words or forms and with the distance from the margins. Remember that the space you leave white is as important as the marks you make.

Keeping a reasonable margin all the way around your sheet is the first means of being sure that your copy has enough "air." The paper sometimes curls and covers up letters that go too close to the margin. Start laying out your sheet by deciding on your margins. *Keep your copy high on the chart* to increase visibility from the back of the room. Leave a deep margin on the bottom. From the back of a room the bottom third of a chart on an easel is often blotted out by the heads of people in the front.

Next lay out your longest line first to get the maximum height of your letters. Experiment on a sheet of regular-size chart paper. If the length of your longest line requires too small or too crowded letters, condense the copy or use two sheets.

You Can Learn to Letter Well

Any style of writing—capitals, lower case (small), or script (handwriting)—will do in most situations, if the sheet is not crowded, the lettering is neat, and the lines are thick enough. Capitals are the easiest letters for most persons to make. Apart from initial caps with lower case, do not mix caps and lower case in one word and rarely in one line. It is generally desirable not to use more than two styles on a sheet.

Thickness of characters, like height, has to be judged by the distance they have to carry. Characters ¼ inch thick will be legible farther away than taller ⅛ inch characters; ½ inch than taller ¼ inch. Varying the width of characters, the ratio of thickness to height, and the space between characters has much to do with why lettering is an art. Experience will show how to adjust proportions for legibility.

On an ordinary flip-chart sheet 12 lines of letters two inches high and ¼ inch thick can be read comfortably from the back of an ordinary small auditorium holding about 200 people. You will find 7 lines more legible and 1 to 3 lines much better for focusing attention. Do not make letters less than 1 inch high for groups up to 50.

Keep size, style, and color of lettering consistent throughout. Avoid making headings excessively larger than the body copy.

Felt-tipped markers are the best instruments for lettering for amateurs. When using felt pens, protect the surface under the sheet from ink seeping through. Keep the tops of the markers on tight when they are not being used.

Experienced letterers also use pens and brushes. In time you should become acquainted with the effects achieved by different instruments and media. The better you understand the elements of typography and design, the more you can contribute to your graphics, even though you do not do the final art work.

You should learn how to make capital letters correctly, even though you never letter by hand with professional skill. The first principle to observe is to follow a consistent style. A little study of the type in any magazine will show that you have four choices—letters of even thickness or thick and thin, and letters with serifs or without serifs. In hand lettering, serifs have little point—in fact, they are often evidence of amateurish fussiness. With the now-standard felt pen with a square point it is as natural to make thick-and-thin strokes as it is strokes of even thickness—for all curved letters it is much easier.

Capital O and S are the hardest letters to make. Learn to make an O first because a good way to start an S is to rough in an O first. Then you have only to learn to join the top and bottom curves with a serpentine diagonal—only. In thick and thin letters the descending strokes are thick. Be sure you observe which of the strokes by convention descend in the M and the N.

If you must do the lettering yourself on charts for important formal presentations—possibly because a professional agency has to charge about $15 an hour—you should look into the various mechanical aids now available. They include stick-on and rub-on alphabets, stencils, tapes, and pantograph devices. On a full-size chart the dull mechanical pantograph lettering needs to be offset by freedom and color in the rest of the design. Rub-on letters require patience to apply, but they give a professionally printed effect.

At times you may wish to create a more immediate effect by writing on a chart as you go along, just as you might on a blackboard. Your audience cannot get ahead of you and may come closer to having a part in your thinking. You will do well to put your material beforehand on the chart lightly in pencil in the proper place and in the proper size. Otherwise you are liable to letter poorly and too small.

Color Adds Interest and Increases Comprehension

A parade of black and white charts seems to lack luster after a while. Color adds sparkle and perks up the interest of the audience. The mere presence of color suggests something more pleasant than a financial report, even though that may be what you are presenting. For this reason discreet tints have been added to the pages of annual printed reports to shareholders, which are written presentations. Charts by commercial artists can be handsome. By using color with restraint on your charts, you can make them more appealing.

But color is functional. It can increase the audience's comprehension of many matters that words explain inadequately and black and white charts only fairly. The most familiar example is the sales chart, where perhaps the graph of past sales, sales trends, and projected sales are all on one sheet. If the lines are all black, the graph is confusing. If the curve of past sales is solid black, sales trends red, and projected sales broken black, the distinctions are obvious, even in a large room—or they are if the lines are thick enough.

Color can communicate in other situations. Flow charts, such as those used to represent manufacturing processes, immigration of peoples, and military campaigns, can be clarified by distinguishing the course of various elements by different colors. Diagrams of such things as a car can be clarified by representing certain parts in bold colors and the rest in neutral ones. Even in simple tabular charts color can pick out items for emphasis and tie together related items, such as, say, the standing of New Jersey on a chart of the states' per capita expenditures for education, welfare, gambling, and cigarets.

Amateur designers, like children, invariably overdo color when they decide to use it. For a beginner a safe rule is to use only one color besides black on a sheet and to stick to that one color throughout. This color might be used for main headings, paragraph spots, related items, or something of the sort.

Color does not always carry well. Some members of every sizable audience are partially or wholly color blind. If you feel you need to use more than one color for major elements, use only boldly contrasting ones, bright red and bright blue or bright green probably being the safest. Orange, purple, and similar gaudy colors may evoke a mood out of key with a serious presentation.

You can get colorful effects quickly by using light-tinted card as a background for dark lettering and dark card for light lettering. *Never* put lettering on any but a strongly contrasting background—never black on red, for instance. White letters on black or dark color are distinctive. By doing one section of a chart on card of a color different from that of the rest of the chart, you can give that section unity and emphasis. Irregular shapes of such sections sometimes add interest.

What has been said about the use of color on charts applies to slides, for slides are often photographs of charts. Even used only as a border, colored card can give slides a professional look. When a slide has substantial blank areas, a tinted background cuts down glare.

Colored adhesive tapes make easy the drawing of straight lines on charts. Adhesive numbers also come in colors.

Overlays, Montage, and Pictographs Introduce Refinements

Sometimes you can communicate complex data visually better by using transparent plastic overlays. For instance, you might present an organization chart first with only the top management and chief division heads listed. Then, after the audience have time to take that in, you can superpose, by means of one or even two overlays, other data related to the various divisions. Flow charts also lend themselves to this treatment.

Unchanging information can be put on transparent plastic, and changing data written on paper beneath the plastic. Material on and under plastic can be photographed for slides. But in such circumstances it is easier to make slides by placing the permanent copy on heavy card, pasting up the changing data temporarily with rubber cement, and then photographing the whole.

One way to liven up your chart presentations without special art work is to cut out appropriate printed words, drawings, or photographs and paste them on card with your copy. This is called *montage*. Use card because paper will wrinkle. Be sure the mounted material is large enough and uncluttered so that it will be clear to the most distant members of the audience. The shape you cut out will often help project the image. Montage can be especially effective on charts that are the basis for slides because color and detail will show up well on a screen.

Pictographs, or ideograms, can be used to turn *quantities* of things into symbols and so make them immediately understandable and differentiated from others on one chart. For instance, it is common to use stylized drawings of little men to represent personnel, toy buildings with tall smoke stacks to represent plants, and coins to represent investment.

Pictographs are often arranged horizontally as bar graphs, with 9½ little men, say, symbolizing 9500 employees and four colored red, perhaps, to represent the 4000 who are under 45 years. The trouble of turning statistical information into pictographs is justified only when an audience might otherwise be confused by your analysis of quantities of several different kinds of things. You can make your own pictographs by tracing appropriate symbols on card and using the cut-out design as a stencil or pattern.

You May Have to Use a Blackboard

The blackboard has been an instrument of instruction for so many generations of teachers that it is almost sacrilegious to question its efficiency. Its size and erasability are assets for small informal presentations. It is handy for spontaneous jotting of figures, formulas, terms, and sketches. One of the best ways to use a blackboard is to write on it in large neat letters or figures beforehand.

For most presentations a blackboard has several defects. The eye-level is often low. What is written on the lower half may be blocked out by the heads of the persons in the front of the room. Visibility of chalk characters on a dusty blackboard is often poor. Some of the new boards are said to be dustless. If the blackboard is attached to a solid wall, the user tends to stand so that he blocks part of the view. If the speaker has to use the blackboard much, he loses his grip on the audience while he stands with his back to them. Few people except school teachers have mastered the trick of writing straight and legibly on a blackboard. Material cannot be prepared in advance, withheld from view, shown at the appropriate point in a presentation, and then withdrawn for later use. It is impossible to make a blackboard presentation visually interesting.

The use of closed-circuit television in universities may lead a few professors to the discovery that it is possible to present material to students by means other than talking at them and scribbling on a blackboard.

Stick-On Boards Fit Certain Occasions

Flannel, flock, magnetic, hook and loop, and similar boards on which you stick, or "slap," letters, whole words, and pictures can be effective in specialized situations. They are best when a talk builds up item by item, each of which can be expressed in a special word or two. Then they provide running notes that aid the listener to follow the presentation point by point. The audience also participates in imagining what will be coming next. Stick-on-board presentations are popular at sales training meetings where formulas for success can be revealed one word at a time.

Stick-on boards have three special advantages: a) They permit the use of printed letters that can be pasted on strips of card to form words, often an improvement over hand lettering. b) They discourage overcrowding. c) They do not tell the audience what you are going to talk about before you get to it, as prepared charts do.

The disadvantages of stick-on boards are: a) They are heavy to carry. b) They involve special set-up time and trouble. c) They create a good deal of motion and turning away from the audience, both of which are distracting except in an emotional presentation. d) They require practice to develop skill in timing in order to get the right effects.

8

Visualizing

Statistical

Information

Graphs Show Quantitative Relationships

Statistical information habitually requires visual presentation. You probably have noticed with dismay how difficult it is to hold in the mind such simple figures as telephone numbers and football scores just from hearing them.

Graphic representation of statistical information for a reader and that for a listener are significantly different. A reader can spend as long as he wants (which is not very long) studying statistical data in a report, a technical article, or a book. A person listening to an oral presentation may not have more than a couple of minutes, possibly only seconds.

Therefore statistical information offered in oral presentation must be much more simplified than in written presentations. Engineers, accountants, market analysts, and others who work with statistics daily often make the serious mistake of using the same statistical tables and graphs for oral presentations that they use in their daily work. Even for an audience of specialists, such graphics are generally improved by simplification.

Audience analysis and situation analysis should determine the right level of complexity and the kind of graphics to use before audiences. The graph of a break-even point in a plant operation can be read in an instant by anyone familiar with such graphs. To a lay audience it might be incomprehensible or require too much time to explain to be worth using.

The handling of statistical information in graphic form is part of the training in most professional disciplines. The process reaches a high degree of mathematical sophistication in many fields. The elementary review that follows is meant to encourage non-technical persons to use appropriate graphic forms when dealing with statistics and to encourage technical persons to simplify the forms they use. Further guidance is at hand in the nearest library.

What an audience wants, we often say, is "the picture." Since it is impossible literally to turn statistical data into graphic images, we mean that graphics afford insight into the most essential inferences to be drawn from the data.

But figures are merely symbolic representations of reality. Just as intentionally or unintentionally figures can misrepresent the truth, so graphics, because they are simplifications of statistics, are peculiarly liable to convey distorted impressions. They are only as dependable as the figures on which they are based, the analysis of those figures, the imagination that gives the analysis a visual form, and the experience of the persons who interpret them. For instance, an unwary person can easily be reassured by a cumulative sales curve merely because it can be shown going up, even when actual sales are below expectation or when cost of sales is too high to yield satisfactory operating margins.

What graphics can reveal more clearly and simply than numbers alone is *quantitative relationships*. Readers and audiences can "realize" how large something is. They can discover what trend is being established. They can appreciate at what rate a trend is progressing and where it will be in the future, if continued at the same rate. They can "see" how much larger something is than something else, how much faster something is progressing than something else, what effect something has on something else, and what will happen in the future if two related trends continue.

Tables Need Not Be Dull

Tables are so standard a part of presentations that they deserve a better fate than usually befalls them. Too often they are regarded as a necessary evil, rather than an important and potentially interesting communication device.

Tables should be titled, dated, and attributed to whoever prepares them. If possible, only those statistics that contribute to the purpose of the presentation should be included. The most significant figures can be given prominence by boxes, color, or similar means.

Two or three tables with a minimum of data are preferable to one of confusing profusion. This is an important truism—important enough for you to remember and observe.

It is easier for the audience to compare figures that are listed vertically. When series are to be compared, they should be placed in parallel juxtaposition. Vertical and horizontal dividing lines in an ink lighter than the figures facilitate the reading of tables.

When you have only a few significant figures to present, you can sometimes record them more comprehensibly by a table than by a graph. You should remember this suggestion after you have simplified for oral presentation data originally plotted on a graph.

Bar Graphs Compare Variations in
Several Sorts of Data

The bar graph is also called a bar chart. The term graph is used here as a reminder that we are discussing the visualizing of statistical information. The bar graph is easy to prepare and easy to understand. Authors of books on statistics make distinctions about different kinds, but not consistently, and accountants and engineers seem to forget the distinctions.

One familiar type of bar graph compares *discrete quantities,* such as the spending of the petroleum industry and that of manufacturing companies. This type compares *separate phenomena.* Therefore the vertical bars have spaces between them. It is sometimes called a *column chart.*

The bar graph can be designed to present a double set of *discrete quantities,* such as the domestic and overseas spending of the petroleum and manufacturing industries. Each bar can be shaded or colored to indicate the domestic and overseas shares of the total spending.

The bar can sometimes more effectively or conveniently present comparisons horizontally. Some authorities limit the term bar graph, or bar chart, to this form.

When a graph uses bars to compare *variables of a single phenomenon,* as financial aid to undergraduates at M.I.T. over the past ten years, the bars have no spaces between them. This type generally records a relatively small number of continuous variables.

By leaving out the vertical bar lines and outlining the mass, a bar graph can give a meaningful quantitative *profile.* It is sometimes called a *contour graph* and is used to show distributions of data, such as population by ages.

If even these rough distinctions give you pause, you had better review the discussion of bar graphs in two or three technical texts. Whatever you elect to do, your bar graphs should be as nearly self interpreting as possible. Otherwise they are not fulfilling their purpose.

Bar graphs lend themselves to bold graphic representation— heavy outlines and strong contrasts. Avoid fidgety cross-hatching and imposed figures that are lost in the background.

Pie Charts Compare Parts of a Whole

The pie chart is a simple way of visualizing *proportionate parts of a whole.* The classic example is a circle representing one dollar divided into wedges to show how money is distributed. The pie chart is ideal for showing percentages when 100 per cent of a whole is accounted for.

Line Graphs Plot Changes in Continuous Data

The line graph, with its familiar zigzags and curves on a grid, is the most common device for visualizing statistical information. Its specal purpose is to plot *continuous data,* such as temperature changes. Thus the line graph records *movement,* frequently in time.

Time Series Record Trends

The most familiar of line graphs is the sales record. For instance, the pounds of plastics sold by a certain plant may be plotted month by month for a year, either cumulatively or not cumulatively. Such sales records can readily be compared with a similar record for the preceding year on the same grid.

Such a graph tells the following at a glance: a) the pounds of plastics sold in a given month to date and in the year before; b) whether the sales in that month are greater or less than those of any other recorded month in either year; c) the trend of the sales for each year; and d) the relationship of the two trends.

This type of graph is relatively simple. Even it can be cluttered up and mishandled so that it detracts from a presentation instead of helping. It is a *time series,* or *historical* graph. It is made up of a series of points, the total sales for each month. They do not stand in a dependent relationship to time—the months do not cause the sales or influence them in any mathematically regular way.

Nevertheless, when such graphic records of experience are kept long enough, a pattern of changes may appear—as seasonal ones in sales and weather or in a sick person's temperature at certain hours. Thus they indicate *trends.* They can be compared with previous records. Then, if you allow for unusual factors, they are of use in forecasting. And they make excellent historical records, for they recall instantly past performances buried in masses of figures.

As a matter of fact, this time series graph is really a bar graph with the tops of the bars connected—a contour graph of sorts. It is continuous only in a relative sense. The fiction that phenomena such as the sales of plastics move from point to point in straight lines helps turn what were long tables of figures into spatial terms that realize essential relationships.

Trends can be indicated by median straight lines or curved lines that smooth out the zigs and zags.

True Line Graphs Record Cause and Effect Interactions

The more complex type of line graph plots the movement of continuous data resulting from the *interaction of two varying phenomena, where one is usually dependent on the other in a functional cause-and-effect relationship.* In such a graph, for instance, you can show how the increase in temperature affects the thermostability of silicone rubber. In this sort of graph the *independent* variables are plotted on the *horizontal* axis (the abscissa), and the *dependent* variables are plotted on the *vertical* axis (the ordinate). The dependent phenomenon—the thermostability of silicone rubber—changes at varying rates as a result of the changes in the independent phenomenon—the temperature. By plotting the reaction of organic rubber to the same temperatures on the same graph, this representation makes visible how much better silicone rubber resists heat than organic rubber does.

The relationship in a true line graph is constant because it presents a mathematically reliable series of data. It is therefore reproducible. If, say, an experiment with a certain rubber has been properly conducted, the relationship of temperature to thermostability for that rubber will always be the same. No such constancy of relationship exists in the time series line graph, except where the phenomena represented are cyclic. That is, a simple linear plotting of regularly recurring events such as sunspots would be dependable for future reference. But the sales during October of one year do not repeat exactly those of the year before or tell certainly what those of the following October will be.

As has been noted, complex line graphs are fit for presentation only to readers with the proper background. They should be translated to the appropriate level of simplification for the brief exposure of an oral presentation for both non-technical and technical audiences. Even then it is usually desirable to explain how they are constructed—at least, what relationships are being shown and what the units of the grid are. The smaller the units, the greater the graphic reaction—that is, a 6 per cent increase will slope upward at a much steeper angle on a monthly grid than on a yearly grid. Grid units should always be as large as circumstances permit.

The use of graphs for technical presentations, oral and written, is infinitely more complex than this simple analysis would suggest. As noted, this simplified account is chiefly meant to encourage the non-technical speaker or writer to use graphs when they will improve his presentation. But it is the technical person who habitually overloads his graphs with secondary data, too many figures, explanatory captions, and lines. So this account also aims at encouraging technical speakers and writers to concentrate on their communication problem and make their graphs effective means of enlightening the listener or reader, not elaborate ends in themselves.

Check Your Graphs by These Ten Questions

1. Do your graphs serve a genuine purpose? Or are they merely something you think might be expected?
2. Is your audience as familiar with graphs as you are? Should you not explain how yours are set up?
3. Do you have so many graphs that they give your presentation an academic tone not in harmony with your overall purpose?
4. Would bar graphs be more effective for some of your data? Have you thought of pictographs?
5. Can you add color to help in visual interpretation of data or to add interest to the graph?
6. Are the lines and lettering on your graphs bold and readable?
7. Can you cut out any material in order to make your design simple and your lines thicker?

8. Are the units on your grid visible and self-evident?
9. Are the figures and legends few, correctly placed, and non-confusing?
10. Have you checked your pencilled layout for accuracy, particularly of spelling, figures, and symbols? Is it final?

9

Slides and

Motion Pictures

For many executives, slides and motion picture presentations are a standard technique. For many more they are a rare or dubious adjunct. Yet the several forms of projection offer so many positive features that you must not fail to study their usefulness for your purposes. For handling graphics before a large audience, projection is nearly mandatory. It also has potential liabilities that you should be familiar with. Most important, you need to learn to capitalize on the independent contributions that projection can make to realize your ideas, and not use it as a mechanical duplication of your text.

Projection Offers Unique Advantages

First of all, projection offers magnification of your graphics. The most common single cause for the failure of presentations is that the audience cannot read the words and figures on charts. The same indictment applies to slides, but it need not. Projection cannot only magnify detail for better visibility; magnification can make certain material more dramatic and interesting. Projection of a photomicrograph of a crystal structure, for instance, represents both virtues.

Projection permits an infinitely greater range of visual material than any other means does. You can illustrate your ideas with any form of graphics—handwritten, printed, drawn, or photographed. You can add sound, including music, noises, and voices besides your own. Your subject matter is limited only by your imagination and pocketbook.

By means of projection you can enrich a presentation with color. The psychological value of this enrichment can be enormous. How dull is an unillustrated talk about birds compared with a motion picture or even slides in color.

A special diffusion-type screen makes it possible to project film and slides from the rear. The image is transmitted *through* the screen. Because it removes the projector and the beam of light from the audience area, rear projection can be used in places where projection would otherwise be impossible.

Rear projection is especially suitable for automatic repeated presentations as in science museums, fairs, and trade shows. It can also be suitable for auditorium presentation, and, in recent miniaturized portable form, even for slides and movies in table-top presentations. The effect is much the same as that of a TV set.

Rear projection does not require a darkened room. Some screen surfaces can be marked up and washed off. The table-top rear projector has wide use for intimate presentations. Carried in a container the size of an attaché case or small suitcase, such a projector can be used in normal light in offices, in conference rooms, and, with imagination, in many situations where audio-visual aids are not ordinarily thought of as feasible.

Motion pictures, of course, can present material far beyond the scope of charts and slides and your unassisted voice. Motion picture film adds movement and continuity of event. Motion pictures document the evidence ... project characters ... tell stories ... create drama ... put great talents at your disposal ... move audiences in ways that you cannot hope to do. Yet the incomparable assistance of motion pictures is often spurned out of vanity, lack of energy, and deficient imagination.

Projection Also Has Limitations

A projector can steal the play from your presentation. What is on the screen inevitably competes with what you are saying. The whir of the projector and the glare of the screen may also introduce a divisive element. When lights go down, you are in danger of becoming a disembodied voice. Your timing and emphasis may be thrown off because you have to take your cue from the screen.

The darkness and the hum from the projector may soothe the audience into drowsiness. When projection takes place in a darkened room, the members of the audience may fail to react as sharply as they do when they are able to see one another. The abrupt change from bright light to dark and back again to light has an irritating effect. It takes the mind of the audience off your presentation.

As noted in Chapter 6, projection can be most effective only when projector, screen, lighting, acoustics, seating, ventilation, and all the other factors of the environment are properly designed and controlled. The technical problems involved are the business of specialists. If you have the interest, however, you can study the effect of the various aspects of projection on presentations and strive for improvement, whether to help yourself or others. The most common forms of projection for presentations—2 x 2 inch (35mm) slides and 16mm film—generally take place in far from ideal surroundings. In your own organization you should do everything in your power to improve conditions in accordance with the suggestions in Chapter 6.

Poor projection conditions are often the results of indifference or ignorance. With just a change or two you can sometimes improve poor arrangements for projection, even when you are making a presentation away from home. You can, for instance, make sure that the room is large enough for the expected audience and that the screen is large enough for the room and the audience.

You may even be able to rearrange the seating according to the formula a) no one closer to the screen than twice the width of the image, and no one farther away, if possible, than six times its width; b) no one outside a 60° angle from the center of the screen

—40° for a beaded screen or for rear projection. One way to decide where the audience should sit is to put a slide on the screen and then sit in different parts of the room.

If you do not have a projection booth, you can cut down on the noise by placing the projector where it ought to be, behind the audience. You can even take advantage of local conditions by home-made stratagems, such as putting the projector just outside the room and poking the lens through the nearly-closed door or between drapes.

You may be able to do something about the light. It is psychologically desirable that the audience have enough light to keep in visual touch with one another. And they should be able to see to take notes—most presentations are meant to generate thoughts. By using a 500 watt lamp projector with forced ventilation, you can project in semi-darkness. New screen fabric, with reflective power much better than that of older screens, helps, too. The best way to obtain semi-darkness is to cut off all the light in the area of the screen and elsewhere except above the audience. But it is not always desirable to keep part of the room lighted. Critical color and fine detail require a room as dark as possible.

The chief complaint about projection is that far too often something mechanical goes wrong. The result can be disastrous. Halfway through a presentation you may find your slides jamming. The heat has made one or more of the cardboard mounts warp. Perhaps, if it is only one, the offender can be pulled out. Otherwise you have to try to finish without slides, an impossibility sometimes. Or suddenly a motion picture film starts acting crazy. A bad splice has caused it to come off the pull-down claws. You had better learn how to handle these mishaps or be sure a trained operator is always sitting beside the machine. Having slides made far enough ahead for early rehearsal should prove whether or not they are functioning well—unless you switch to a different model projector for your actual presentation.

When your presentation, or one that you are responsible for, depends on slides or film, do not accept assurances lightly about the readiness of the equipment or the expertness of the projectionist. In any situation where projection failure would have serious results, perhaps ruin your presentation entirely, insist on having an experienced projectionist check the equipment well in advance and be on hand during your presentation—close at hand.

When you are going to use an unfamiliar projector, make certain in advance that it will accept your film, mount, or magazine. If your film has a sound track, be sure that the projector is equipped for sound. Different makes and models of slide projectors vary annoyingly in what they can handle. Take the trouble to be sure a spare lamp is beside the projector and that someone, including you, knows how to install it. And while you are double-checking details, when you take your own projector with you to an unfamiliar room, throw in a good long extension cord. A plug may not be handy.

An electric pointer is useful when you cannot satisfactorily use an ordinary one. But you must practice using it until you can hold the spot or arrow precisely and steadily on the detail you want the audience to note. A wavering, jumping lighted spot or arrow is a nuisance, not a help.

Projectors of all types are expensive. Until you are certain that you will use one type regularly enough to justify its purchase by your organization, you should rent. Then you can test different models—and your seriousness about using projection. Technical assistance cannot always be available, particularly on trips. Nontechnical persons often become bored with the preparatory chores, mechanical attentions, and frustrations that are part of using projectors. Or because they are non-technical, all machinery makes them nervous. They stop using projectors. Then expensive equipment sits idle.

Therefore, to get the best results from projection, learn its good and bad points. Then you will know either enough to take care of the problems yourself or have someone do it for you. Or you will sometimes wisely decide that the visual element in a presentation does not justify the attention that has to be devoted to projection to make it calamity-proof.

Slides Have Great Versatility

The choice between charts and slides for formal small-group presentations has become hard to make, now that projection equipment has improved a great deal in the last few years. Slides are much easier to carry around than charts are, and they can be mailed with less trouble. Changing slides can sometimes be less distracting than handling charts.

But in some situations charts will be tolerated when slides or film will not be. Setting up a projector in someone's office, for example, may seem presumptuous. Charts seem more suitable for informal occasions. They can be quickly put together by anyone, if the occasion demands. Slides require technical processing. Charts do not break down; projectors do.

Yet by means of slides you can present all of the material that you can put on charts, and much that you cannot. You can use all of the color that you wish—whereas just one photograph blown up to chart size might cost you $50. The preparation of graphs and other copy for slides may cost less or more than for charts. The cost depends not only on the kind of copy and who does the work, but also on your understanding of what is involved in making slides. The cost of slides is often excessive because the person making the presentation has never thought about the difference between written copy and slides.

Slides can be projected on conference tables and in big auditoriums. They can easily be rearranged for different audiences and time schedules, and they can be up-dated with almost no effort. A major convenience is that slides can be carried and filed without trouble, and they stay in perfect condition indefinitely, unless someone's fingerprints smudge them. Therefore they are popular with professional speakers, especially those who travel and repeat the same presentation, or the same basic one adjusted to local conditions.

The projection of 2 x 2 inch slides is now so satisfactory that you will find little justification for 3¼ x 4 inch glass lantern slides. They used to be mandatory for slide projection in auditoriums, but with improved film and projectors you will find 2 x 2 inch slides fit normal presentation situations, up to 200 persons. A standard 2 x 2 inch slide projector fitted with a 9 or 10 inch focal-length lens and a 500 watt lamp can be used from the back of an auditorium. Or 2 x 2 inch slides can be projected from a 3¼ x 4 inch lantern slide projector fitted with an adaptor.

The projector for 3¼ x 4 inch slides is too heavy to carry around, and it almost always requires manual feeding of slides. One is usually available with an adaptor in hotels, technical society auditoriums, and other places where slide presentations to large audiences are common. Color slides of 3¼ x 4 inch size must be specially ordered from custom processing laboratories and are much more expensive than are 2 x 2 inch slides. Lantern slides can be hand colored, but this process has limited applications. It, too, is expensive. Polaroid has a process for making inexpensive black-and-white slides of excellent quality in a matter of two minutes. When preparation time is at a premium, this process might save your presentation. Polaroid is working on a color transparency process. When it is available, slide presentations will become much more convenient.

Slides Must Be Properly Projected

Manual slide projectors have the disadvantage of either requiring you to signal an operator when to shift the image or else to stand with your back to part of the audience while you try to talk and run the gadget yourself.

If you are using slides often for presentations, you should procure a projector with a remote control. Then you can stand in front of your audience and shift slides without having either to hunch over the projector or keep saying, "Next slide, please," to an operator. A remote control can start the projector, turn it off, reverse slides, and focus them. There are also random access controls that permit the selective viewing of slides. Not being tied to a set sequence could be an asset in certain presentations and in question-and-answer periods.

A thorough rehearsal should teach you how to use a remote control. The usual blunders of the novice are to keep his thumb on the control a bit too long and go past his slide or to reverse instead of going forward.

You can use a remote control even in an auditorium, although not usually with 3¼ x 4 inch projectors. But since an auditorium-sized audience indicates an important occasion, you should, as already suggested, have a competent technician on hand, whether or not you use a remote control.

With a little experience you will almost always want to use remote control for slide presentations. It not only eliminates the distraction of breaking your discourse while you change slides or of communicating with a projectionist; it gives you split-second control of your timing. It should reduce the possibility that you will leave a slide on the screen too long or talk about matter unrelated to the slide being shown. But only keeping your wits about you will really prevent these two tiresome bloopers.

If you must use a projectionist, rehearse painstakingly with him. He should become so familiar with your material that he knows as well as you do when you are finished with one slide and need the next. If at all possible, agree on visual signals not voice or noise commands.

Speakers sometimes put several complete summary sentences on slides. Instead of being cues, they are complete thoughts. Then while the members of the audience are trying to absorb with their ears what the speaker is saying, with their eyes they are reading different ideas on the slides. They cannot help it. No one can sit staring at words on a lighted screen without reading them. The result is the confusion of divided attention. Several items should be put on one slide only when you proceed briskly from one to another. If you are going to talk about each for several minutes, put each on a separate slide.

Spacing your slides is important. You should have enough slides so that most of the time you are talking about what they show. Or you should concentrate on the ones you have so that you can talk steadily about them and then cut off the projector and turn the lights on. Or, less desirably, you should cut off the projector and turn on the lights between slides. One or two such maneuvers are all that an audience should stand. If you project on a screen that is in a darkened area while you keep the room lights on, you can cut off the projector with less commotion than if you have to turn the lights on, too.

What you do *not* want to do is to have the audience reading the copy on one slide even for a minute after you have finished with it and gone on to something else. Nor do you want to have them sit staring at a blinding blank lighted screen between slides. And of course you do not want the audience studying a slide before you get to it.

Be sure your slides are numbered in the proper sequence and inserted in the right position. One upside-down slide can make an audience laugh just as you are making a serious point. A mix-up in order can be a calamity and destroy your poise. Preview your slides in time to catch mistakes and omissions and to have new slides made if necessary. Errors cannot be corrected on slides, remember. No audience will ever forgive a speaker who admits he has not bothered to check his slides beforehand.

You may have no control over projection conditions, but you can bear these viewing problems in mind, both when you are giving a presentation with slides and when you are preparing them. Slides must be properly projected to be effective.

Follow These Suggestions for Preparing Slides

In the preparation of slides much the same rules apply as in the making of charts, but even greater care must be taken to avoid crowding. If the slide is too complicated, you may lose the attention of your audience while they are trying to sort out the information on the slide.

Paradoxically, it is more usual to crowd slides than charts. The reason is that slides can be photographed from typed copy. They therefore often contain secondary and non-essential material as well as primary and essential. The ease of transfer is a fatal block to simplifying copy to meet the realities of the situation. Typed copy on slides is habitually too small. To make matters worse, the copy for a 2 x 3 (horizontal) format is too often typed on 8½ x 11 inch (vertical) paper.

Pantograph lettering is appropriate on slides for technical presentations. Electric typewriters are now equipped with changeable fonts so that you can specify larger letters and bold-face letters when you want them. As noted in Chapter 7, rub-on letters look like professional printing. But the verve of hand lettering on full-scale charts can be transferred to slides and is often preferable to mechanical lettering for general-purpose talks.

To make a slide, your copy has to be photographed. Careful observation of what happens in the reduction should guide you in establishing proper heights and thicknesses for the lettering on your copy. Different types and sizes of audiences make some flexibility possible.

Slides conforming to the following standards can be comfortably read under ordinary conditions: a) For 2 x 2 inch (35mm) slides keep your copy within a rectangle with a 2 x 3 horizontal ratio. *Allow for adequate margins.* Your master can then be photographed without cropping. The 2 x 3 horizontal ratio comes from the fact that the actual size of the opening on a 2 x 2 (35mm) slide is 24 x 36mm. (If you use 2 x 2 *superslides,* however, the format is square.) You risk having your slides run off the screen unless you stick strictly to the 2 x 3 ratio in a *horizontal* format. Mixing in vertical formats is distracting to the audience and often results in rags and tatters of your carefully prepared material on the floor and ceiling. b) The minimum letter height for copy for slides is ⅛ inch, better ¼ inch, on 4 x 6 inch paper. Copy and art work on chart-size paper look well when reduced for slides. (See chapter 7 for keeping reductions and enlargements in proportion.) Do not forget that *lettering* on charts or other large rectangles must be correspondingly enlarged in order to reduce in proportion. The space between lines of copy should also be sufficient so that reduction does not squeeze lines together.

When preparing copy for slides, use India ink. Many societies have rules against typewritten slides, but by using an electric typewriter with a carbon ribbon, legible slides can be produced. Slides with a large amount of white space produce an annoying glare. As noted elsewhere, to avoid glare, use tinted paper or card for your original copy. Different tints give a pleasing variety. Or you can cut out your copy and paste it on tinted card. Sometimes a mat of color will make black and white copy look rich.

Some speakers prefer to use negative slides—that is, light letters on a dark background. This reduces glare and eyestrain and increases visibility when some of the room lights are left on. These slides can also be colored. If negative slides are used, the letters and characters should be thin in proportion to their size, because the optical phenomenon of halation makes them look thicker on the screen. Conversely, lettering on positive slides should be thicker because halation will tend to make them look thin.

In using photographs on slides, you have to be sure that you do not include irrelevant detail. If you are taking your own photographs, therefore, focus only on that object or area that you are discussing and fill your slide with it. If your only photograph does include distracting detail, mask out the portion you do not need and re-photograph. Sometimes you can add arrows, letters, or other indicators as cues for the audience. You cannot edit the slide itself.

When your presentation is built around a not easily memorized list of, say, five or more headings, you might repeat the slide of the whole list as you begin a new heading. As the copy is re-photographed each time, move an arrowhead pointer to the heading to be discussed. This simple device prevents confusion and reinforces the audience's memory of the entire list.

Glass mounts are best for 2 x 2 inch slides. Cardboard-mounted slides have to be individually focussed and are easily damaged. *Thin* glass mounts should be used with *remote control.* Standard glass mounts are too thick, and cardboard mounts heat up, buckle, and jam. You will be sorry if you ignore this suggestion. You might also investigate the new plastic mounts.

The cost of preparing slides depends first on *whether the copy submitted is ready to be photographed or whether rough copy must be turned into a master.*

If the copy can be photographed, the variables are the size of the slide, whether or not it is to be glass mounted, and whether or not hand coloring of negative slides is required. Such costs can run from half a dollar a slide to a charge for labor by the hour.

If the rough copy must be turned into a master, then you start with the labor cost, which may be $5 or $6 an hour inside an organization and three or four times that outside. How much time one slide will take depends on how much creative art work it requires. It can take several hours just to turn a single graph of the technical properties of a product into a presentable slide. You can see why a charge of $100 for ten slides might not be unusual.

Turn your copy over to be processed into slides as far as possible in advance of your presentation. Whoever does it has other work to do. If you fail to allow two or three weeks, you may wind up with a crisis on your hands. While this is habitual, it is unintelligent. You should allow time for careful work, time for correction or addition, and time for rehearsal with the slides and projection equipment that you will use.

Motion Picture Films Widen the Scope of Presentations

A film can span space and time in a way that is at once natural and compressed. Suppose you wish to make a presentation to a city council to urge the desirability of a downtown rehabilitation program. You could show scenes from several cities before and after rehabilitation and in different seasons. Such visualization, supplemented by taped interviews, would convey a sense of reality that would be much more persuasive than a facts-and-figures talk alone.

Even more compellingly, film can throw an aura of interest about any subject. Color and motion are attention getters and interest holders. They introduce elements altogether beyond the reach of talk alone.

One advantage of a film is that it is prepared in advance of a presentation and is worked over and edited until it is satisfactory. Then, except for the possibility of equipment trouble, you can be sure of duplicating this part of your presentation exactly every time. In selling, for instance, where 100 different salesmen may make the same presentation over and over, a film can be a guarantee of consistency, accuracy, and level of quality.

Or suppose your company manufactures musical instruments. You want the public to identify your company as the leader in the field. You might well consider spending $100,000 for a 28-minute film that would include something about the history of musical instruments, the manufacture of musical instruments today (filmed in your plant, of course), and criteria for judging the value of an instrument, all with passages of good music along the way played by well-known artists. Such a film would be welcomed by schools and colleges, by commercial as well as educational television stations, and by clubs. In addition, with luck, it could be a standard part of your public relations and sales promotion for years.

If you work for an industrial corporation, the government, a university, or other large organization, you will often have access to films produced by that organization. And an audio-visual department will try to get what you need, if someone else has produced it. Hundreds of fine films are available free from industrial firms and government agencies and for rental at reasonable fees from other sources. For advice see your local librarian or inquire at the nearest university or educational TV station.

You will occasionally use a film as your whole presentation. These films may have narrative and sound effects on a separate sound track. If you are a supervisor, you may wish to use one of your personnel department's films for training purposes. If you are a salesman or applications engineer presenting a product to customers, you may rely mainly on a film produced for the purpose.

In instances of this sort, a brief introduction may be desirable in orienting the audience—who produced the film, what its message is, what points to look for especially. For training or sales use, follow-up discussion is necessary to emphasize main points and answer questions.

A film may be only part of a presentation, a means of covering background material before you begin your specialized talk. A representative of a travel agency might first offer a film of the highlights of a trip to the Holy Land before making an appeal to a church group to organize a tour. Or, another possibility, an engineer might explain the technical aspects of a new synthetic fiber while a silent film pictures the steps in its manufacture.

You should a) carefully preview a film before you show it; b) make sure it is up to date and in good shape; c) when it is only background, be certain its setting up and running time will not eat up time you must have for your presentation proper; d) make certain *in advance* that you will have both the right equipment and an operator to handle your film. If you must operate the projector, be sure that you know how and what to do in case it fails to work properly.

Projectors that can be slowed, sped up, halted, and reversed are now available. A motion picture can therefore be stopped for discussion of a particular frame or passage. On older projectors the film cannot be so manipulated. If you have to skip around, as in a question and answer period or a teaching situation, slides may be preferable or may be used for discussion after a motion picture presentation.

You should have little difficulty about using a professionally prepared motion picture, as long as you or someone else knows how to operate the projector. Even then you have to be on guard that you do not turn up somewhere with a sound film when the projector handles only silent film.

Making a Motion Picture Is Expensive

Making your own motion picture film to meet special needs is another matter. Many organizations have photographic units able to produce a passable motion picture. At least they are able to put together something like a training film or one to go with a Community Chest campaign. For some presentations—about nature and travel, for instance—an amateur film may be excellent, especially if certain technical operations are handled by a professional service firm. But only professional producers normally have the necessary resources and experience to produce a motion picture for wide distribution, such as one for national sales promotion or for corporate identity purposes.

Having a motion picture made by a professional studio is not something to be undertaken lightly. Professional motion picture making is a composite of art, experience, intricate technology, logistics, cost accounting, and human relations. A reputable motion picture maker may charge $500 to $2000 or more for each minute of running time of a film. The cost of animation may run three times as high. Only assurance of exposure to millions of people or to extremely significant audiences—the alumni clubs of a university for a fund-raising film—can justify such initial expense. Prints and distribution charges can run into several thousand dollars more. And one change, as of a product model or the president of the university, can kill the film.

The wide variation in cost estimates of film-makers reflects to some degree their professional standing and the salary, wages, and other overhead costs in different studios and parts of the country. But it also reflects the difference in how they interpret your statements of what you want. The basic concepts in the scripts of two producers, for instance, may be far apart in the demands made on their crews, in the number, experience, and roles of the actors, and the amount of shooting that has to be done on location.

A low estimate may represent one producer's intention to piece out passages with stills, stock film, such as that available from the armed forces, or footage he has left over from other films. Another producer might feel original photography a necessity. A high estimate may include the commissioning of original music or the use of a famous orchestra; a lower bid may mean that music already available will be used.

Yet higher costs do not ensure a better motion picture. Original music is not necessarily better for a specific picture than music already recorded, nor, for that matter, is music necessarily better than no music. An intelligent narrator with a suitable voice can add a great deal to a motion picture presentation. Yet a "name" narrator may increase costs $5000 and merely seem an intruder.

In certain circumstances a desirable alternative to going out and making personal presentations or having a motion picture made is to work out a program with a television station. You can have a video tape for use on TV stations made from a live program. From the video tape you can have a relatively inexpensive black and white kinescope made for regular motion picture projection. The quality is usually not up to regular motion picture film standard, but techniques are improving. Kinescopes in color should be readily available in the future.

The Sponsor Must Contribute to the Motion Picture

If you are in charge of having a motion picture made for presentation purposes, you must take the responsibility for it and devote a great deal of time to doing your part of the job. Or else you should delegate the responsibility—and not second-guess the person to whom you have given the assignment, whether he works for your organization or is an outside producer.

If you have primary responsibility for deciding on having a motion picture made, you *must* be able to answer two basic questions: a) *What definable group are you trying to influence?* b) *What do you want each member of that group to remember or do after viewing your film?*

This sounds simple, yet producers have trouble prying unequivocal answers from sponsors. Much of the difficulty lies in the fact that, as in any other presentation, the message must be crystal clear and involve no more than three or four related ideas. "Because it is strong, light, and easily cut, Metallix is excellent for construction. It can be used for siding on houses, for building boats, and for jobs around the house." Something of this sort is all that a home audience could be expected to remember from a film. If the film also tries to tell what the molecular structure of Metallix is, the story of its invention, and who the president of Metallix Corporation is, the audience will miss the essential message.

What often happens, especially in corporate films, is that the sponsor will not define his audience and limit his film to one message. The reason is that films often embody inharmonious suggestions from several persons who look at the enterprise from different points of view. In our not-so-imaginary Metallix film, for instance, it would be natural that the director of research consider an explanation of the molecular structure of Metallix and the story of its invention supremely interesting, while the assistant to the president might recommend a scene or two in the president's office—"to show what kind of people we are here at Metallix Corporation." In this stereotyped situation what presumably should be a straight product-promotion film is thrown out of focus by elements of educational and corporate identity films.

Alas, the alternative is not, as producers devoutly wish, for you to turn the whole thing over to a producer and then keep out of the way. Many producers sincerely believe that they can do a satisfactory film after a week or so of talking to people in an organization, reading relevant material, and observing. They probably can if the subject is hubcaps or helicopters. In dealing with more complex subjects, they may do films satisfactory to themselves and to judges of film festivals, and yet miss the target in the judgment of persons with insight into the subject.

The best part of most presentation films is the photography. The weakest is the script. Many industrial films represent a high level of photographic virtuosity—sometimes even artistic excellence—dedicated to commonplace concepts.

A film, like any other form of literary art, is only as good as the concepts from which the script grows. Educational, training, and sales films tend to be satisfactory because they stick to simple central concepts. Corporate identity films tend to be artistically bad because they try to cover too much ground, or because the producer shows off his bag of tricks to cover up the banality of the script—or both.

Beneath the surface the trouble usually is that the writer has been driven to pretentiousness in an effort to dress up the prosy thinking of the sponsors. If, therefore, you seek an original, exciting film to be your presentation, you have to start by contributing some hard, sensitive, informed, imaginative thinking yourself. You can leave the producer to his own devices but not to his own thinking. You have to engage in a thoughtful partnership with him.

Animation Can Add Zest to a Motion Picture

For certain purposes animation can heighten the effectiveness of a film presentation. Animation is commonly known for comic presentations, but it can be serious. It consists of drawings, paintings, photographs, or objects that seem to move. This illusion is created by photographing them and their parts in a sequence of slightly changed positions, as in a Donald Duck film—in other words, by simulating a moving picture. Speech and music are synchronized with the images, as desired.

Movement can also be simulated in part or wholly by moving the camera or the art work or an inanimate object. This inexpensive technique often is remarkably convincing and interesting.

Animation as a serious presentation form has made much progress in the last few years. It is possible to turn an inescapably routine situation—why the manufacturers of aerospace materials

should advertise in a certain aerospace magazine—into an atten-
tion-holding film by means of a humorous narrative acted out by
diverting animation. If the contents are imaginative, a clever
animation artist can make presentation points with a drollery that
breaks down resistance. Diagrammatic animation can clarify the
structure and action of complex mechanisms and processes. It can
also give life to comparisons of quantities, as by adding the units
of a bar graph in sequence.

Animation can add an element of beauty, fantasy, or charm
not possible to duplicate by other means. Its effectiveness often
depends on the fact that it is art, not life. Sometimes animation
can visualize action and concepts that cannot be handled convincingly by living actors and real scenes—what happens to spacecraft after take-off, for instance. Sometimes it can do what would
otherwise be prohibitively expensive, such as scenes in remote
places using large numbers of professional actors. The research
and art work that can go into animation sometimes makes it ex-
traordinarily expensive. Yet if you are thinking about a film presentation, you should consider the contribution that animation
might make.

10

Other

Audio-Visual Aids

In addition to the standard slides and motion picture film, you will on occasion find use for other forms of projection and other kinds of audio-visual aids. These other forms are meant for use in special circumstances where regular charts, slides, and motion pictures may seem not so applicable. They therefore tend to be less familiar to many speakers. Many shun them entirely; others use them awkwardly; and still others misuse them. You should know enough about them to be able to select the occasion when one form can serve you better than another.

Sound Film Presentations
Can Be Made on a Table Top

A presentation often is an intimate affair. Sometimes the more important it is, the more intimate. Such presentations invariably take place in offices or other limited quarters. In the past many persons have yearned to use sound film in such circumstances for special occasions. But it has not always been possible to lure an audience of three, four, or one to a projection room; it has been impossible to lug a 16mm projector and screen into cramped quarters. Even an 8mm "family" projector and screen would cause too much undignified disturbance. Anyway 8mm film was only for hobbyists. Its quality was not satisfactory for professional purposes, and it was silent.

The recent development of high quality 8mm sound color film together with rear-screen projection has changed this presentation situation. Lightweight units can be placed on a table or desk-top, plugged in, and a color film with sound presented on a foot-square screen in the unit. This is made possible by rear-screen projection and also by new film cartridges designed for these table-top projectors. The cartridge requires no attention—in fact, no hand can touch the film. Insert it into the projector like a piece of toast. Flip a switch, and you have both excellent image and sound.

The width of ordinary recording tape, 8mm film is convenient for handling, carrying, and mailing. Apart from its obvious aid to office sales presentations, this 8mm sound film cartridge projector can have a tremendous effect on teaching. Small groups of students or individuals are able to draw out cartridges as they would a book and study a film related to a course, without a teacher's presentation. For larger groups the cartridge can also be used for front projection. If necessary, the sound can be heard through head phones. All that is needed to have this relatively inexpensive device improve school and college teaching throughout the land is to have the vast store of wonderful educational films already in existence made available on 8mm film. What it could do to extend library services teases the imagination.

A Filmstrip May Be Just What You Need

A variant of slides and film is the filmstrip, or slidefilm. It is made up of stills—photographs or art, with or without color. They are photographed on frames of 35mm film in a continuous roll. Captions can be added to an original photograph. Filmstrips may be accompanied by sound on tape or records. Automatic operation, plus enlargement and clarity of detail, gives the filmstrip a special usefulness where the same message must be presented many times. It can also be operated by hand and stopped for discussion of a single frame.

Some filmstrip projectors are fairly primitive, but better ones come along each year. When you have a presentation based on a lot of slides, you might have them turned into a filmstrip. Suppose you are a salesman selling a machine not yet in production. You could show working drawings and photographs of models, and you could talk along as the images appear, or you could have a tape-recorded explanation by the designer. This is the inexpensive method. A master negative and one print might cost a minimum of $25 plus $1 a frame.

But a filmstrip can be a much more sophisticated, and expensive, presentation. You can engage a professional studio to write a special script, with an expert narrator to fit it to the images. The synchronizing of such a narration with the filmstrip and the mixing of music and other sound effects becomes a complex technical job. A professional studio might charge $5000 to prepare a 10 minute filmstrip with a sound track. But 100 units can then be reproduced for $500–$1000. Thus 100 salesmen can be provided with a sales promotion device to enhance thousands of presentations.

By means of automatic devices, filmstrip presentations can be repeated over and over. For instance, a hardware store can be furnished with a week-long promotion without requiring live presentation. At a trade show a filmstrip with sound can present a manufacturer's story to the passing crowd hour after hour, while the salesmen at a booth talk to potential customers.

Filmstrips are widely used for sales and training presentations. For instance, in a plant a filmstrip made from photographs and drawings of a complex machine can be a basic tool in the training of new operators. In selling, filmstrips are especially popular as desk- and table-top sales aids, with either front or rear projection. Some are battery powered to avoid the need of plugging in a cord. Even a silent filmstrip is more effective in arousing interest than shuffling through the same photographs or whatever graphics may be the subjects of the stills. Color filmstrip is, moreover, livelier and truer than printed color photographs.

One advantage of filmstrip is that the order of the presentation remains unchanged. It is not subject to rearrangement by accident or somebody's whim as slides are. On the other hand, if you wish to make any change, you must make another filmstrip.

Overhead Projectors Show Copy from Transparencies

An overhead projector projects copy that has been put on plastic transparencies. The transparency is placed flat on a glass surface strongly lighted from below, and the image is reflected by the projection mirror and lens assembly held overhead by a vertical upright. The usual machine is portable and projects from table height a short distance from the screen.

The transparencies are in effect slides. They are inexpensive and come in three sizes—5 x 5 inches, 7 x 7 inches, and for full-size screens 10 x 10 inches. You must, as always, allow a) for margins and b) for the greatest distance from which the letters or figures must be readable.

The overhead projector has virtues that make it suitable for certain situations. It can be used in normal light for black and white, though the image is much better with the screen area dark. The screen must be dark for sharp detail and critical color. Once the projector, screen, and audience are properly placed—a matter of considerable importance—the operation is simple and free from mechanical troubles. Normally, you do not need an operator or stand-by technician.

You can stand or sit beside the overhead projector, face the audience, and take your cue from notes written on the margin of the transparencies. You can write or draw on the transparencies and point to specific spots on them as you talk. By means of overlays, you can build up slides, mask out sections, and even simulate motion.

Except for the preparation of unusual art work, overlays, and color effects, the overhead projector is an inexpensive device to operate. It can also circumvent the delay necessary for the processing of ordinary slides.

Suppose that you are a company controller who has to give financial reports at least once a month to a dozen of your execu-

tive colleagues. What are your choices? You can pass around
copies of your material. Then the room is full of the rustle of
paper. Your colleagues get lost or stray away to page 7 and do
not listen while you talk about page 2. Or you can have your
pages of figures and graphs laboriously put on charts or slides by
an audio-visual department. This takes time that you usually do
not have, and it may compromise the security of confidential information. Or you can have the various financial reports, just as
they come to you—often necessarily at the last minute—reproduced on transparencies by your own office copier. In a few minutes your graphics are ready for your presentation.

Overhead projectors have disadvantages. Unless you place the
projector just right in relation to the screen and the audience, a
"keystone" distortion take place. Tripod, wall, pull-down, and
rear screens present different problems. Often a tilted pulldown
screen is best.

The ease with which original sheets of typed material and
graphs can be reproduced on transparencies without change is a
temptation not to bother to select and simplify and emphasize.
Transparencies must be placed under the lens and changed by
hand. This manual busy-work may distract the audience and,
worse, divide the attention of the speaker. He tends to forsake
the audience and his text and to break his rhythm with stuttery
pauses.

Worse, since the machine must be on a table or stand near the
screen, both it and the operator are usually in the center between
the audience and the screen. The audience thus tends to divide
into two side groups, an awkward arrangement for a speaker, and
a psychologically unsatisfactory one for the audience. If the
speaker stands up, he blocks the screen. If he sits, he is unim-
pressive. Angle projection and rear projection are possible.

In using an overhead projector, the speaker tends to turn his
back on part of the audience to follow the copy on the screen.
And he stares down into the glare at the transparencies and his
side notes. In the strongly contrasting lighting he looks strange
and apart from the audience, like a gypsy fortune teller reading
tea leaves. Unless he rests his pencil on the transparency when he

is pointing, the pencil shakes as though he has palsy. When he writes on the transparency, he blocks out the image on the screen. Such writing, therefore, must be practised in order to do it quickly.

As with all projection, it is important to use the overhead projector, not let it use you. That means especially that you put on the transparency what is peculiarly suited to help convey your message and not compete with what you are saying. In general the overhead projector seems better suited for small-group explanatory presentations than for persuasive ones.

Opaque Projectors Need No Processing of Copy

Also by means of a mirror and lens assembly, an opaque projector permits you to project images of printed or typed copy, graphs, drawings, maps, and photographs directly from the actual material. This material can be in color. It must be flat, thin, opaque, and no larger than typewriter-paper size.

The advantage of not having to bother with slides, film, or even transparencies—to be able to flash MS, figures, maps, chemical formulas, drawings, or colored photographs on a screen without processing them in any way—is sometimes a great one. It is certainly a time-saver and cost-saver.

The opaque projector can be a useful aid in some teaching presentations, as in accounting or machine design, where student work can be analyzed visually. No other device meets this special situation as well as the opaque projector does.

The opaque projector has serious disadvantages. You must operate it in darkness. You and the audience lose contact, and the audience cannot see to take notes. The opaque projector does not give sharp definition. The machine is bulky and not yet readily portable. It projects from close to the screen. Therefore you and it may block the view of the screen. You usually have to adjust the copy as you insert it. Finally, the very lack of need to prepare special material is a temptation to use crowded written copy in un-unified form.

In brief, the opaque projector seems better adapted to the study of visual material by a small group than to a normal presentation.

Public Address Systems Are Indispensable

In spite of their often undependable behavior, public address systems contribute a great deal to the success of many of your presentations. Without amplification, your voice may not be heard in all parts of rooms with poor acoustics, or it may be heard only part of the time, or it may at least lose its resonance and authority. In a "dead" room a public address system is desirable if more than 50 are in the audience. If you have to move about, or if you like to move about, a necklace microphone is your answer. But resist the temptation to turn and wander around needlessly and distractingly.

Sound systems are the business of engineers and technicians. Amplifiers, loud speakers, and microphones, whether portable or permanent, should be selected, installed, and maintained by experts. In general, if you want the best results, you have to pay for expensive equipment. But the proper placement of the units of the equipment, their adjustment in relation to the idiosyncrasies of the room, and the way you use the microphone can have a decisive effect on how your voice sounds. A satisfactory sound system is one that avoids distortion when you run amplifiers and speakers below maximum volume.

An extremely useful innovation is a portable lectern-amplifier. Transistorized and battery-powered, it has a reading light and both a stationary microphone and a necklace attachment. It has one built-in speaker and another can be placed in another part of the room. The unit is extremely light. It not only provides a lighted reading stand for script or notes where one might not be available; it also offers a full-strength public address system.

The amplifier and speakers can mean the difference between success and a weak presentation. Their special usefulness is not merely in large rooms or outdoors where no public adddress system is provided. Two other common enemies of good presentations are poor acoustics in a moderate-sized room and the noise of a slide or motion picture projector in a conference room. In rooms of these types, public address systems are rarely found. In both, your voice can lose vigor and resonance by the time it reaches the ears of persons ten or fifteen feet away. The portable lectern-amplifier allows you to adjust the volume of your voice so that it sounds natural and strong. Any speaker who makes many presentations in unpredictable surroundings ought to have a portable lectern-amplifier as a standard part of his equipment.

On television and before large gatherings, a Teleprompter may seem an improvement over reading from a script. It is a compact electrical unit that can be carried in a suitcase and placed on a lectern or in front of it. It unrolls words in letters 8 times typewriter size. The speaker can control the speed of the Teleprompter and stop it. It takes experience to use one and look at the audience, too. Most users look hypnotized.

How Can You Use Recordings?

You will sometimes use recordings in one form or another as an adjunct to a presentation. You might conceivably record your entire presentation for someone else to deliver. You might wish to introduce material recorded earlier, as an interview, bird-songs, or different dialects in a presentation about regional speech. Or you might have someone who cannot be present—the governor of a state during an election, for instance—address the audience through a recording.

You are more likely to use the tape recorder than any other sound device. You might conceivably use available phonograph records for some appropriate purpose—World War II speeches in a history class. You might have a phonograph record especially made for any purpose where sound is needed, as to accompany a filmstrip. But since only professional recording studios have the equipment to make phonograph records and anyone can use a tape recorder, tape has become the universal sound medium. Tape is used as the first recording of the narrative that accompanies most professional film and filmstrip presentations. Tape can be corrected easily, and it can be erased and used over and over.

For rehearsals and informal presentations, a standard monaural recorder and the microphone that comes with it are adequate. For more ambitious purposes, a high-quality—i.e., expensive— recorder and microphone are necessary. For all purposes only the best quality of tape is recommended.

With experience you probably can edit simple taped sound presentations to synchronize with your own slide or filmstrip visuals. But the making of a true film sound track is an intricate procedure best left to professionals.

Since almost everyone has a record player, you may have a professional studio put a presentation on a vinyl or paper record for free mailing.

A common use of the tape recorder is for play-back and analysis of group discussion following a presentation, as during sales and management training courses. If you try something of this sort, be sure a) that you have a good microphone, b) that the volume is set properly, c) that members of the group are near enough for their voices to be clear, and d) only one person speaks at a time. To be sure of these things, you should either use a monitor or make a short trial and then start over. A tape recorder is a reliable device, once you become used to it.

Putting your talk on a tape and then listening to yourself is one of the best ways of preparing for a presentation. You probably do not know what your voice sounds like. It is often a shock to hear how you sound to others—or approximately so, since only expensive tape recorders are free of distortion. Hearing yourself may be all you need to stop talking through your nose, saying *uh,* or whatever your speech idiosyncrasy may be—and you have one or more. A tape recorder gives you a chance to practice correcting the weaknesses you notice. Having an experienced critic comment while you listen to yourself is a good idea, too.

By making your presentation to a tape recorder, you can get something of the feel of the occasion itself. The mere turning of the reels and the knowledge that your voice is being recorded goad you to keep talking. You can then time yourself precisely—except that you will usually take less time in doing a tape than in talking to a live audience. In using a tape recorder for rehearsal you can go over and over your presentation, until you are certain that it flows as logically and persuasively and urbanely as you know it should.

Portable Video-Tape Recorders Show Promise

Recently introduced portable video-tape records seem to open new opportunities for the rehearsal of presentations, rather than for presentations. These sets, complete with camera, recorder, and monitor now sell for about $1000. They record (black and white) sight and sound together on magnetic tape. Such do-it-yourself video-tape cannot match the quality of that made in a TV studio. Nor can it match the quality and versatility of a sound film. But it will make economically feasible certain activities formerly almost out of reach.

A portable video-tape recorder has three important advantages. First, it offers the convenience of visual and sound recording of a rehearsal in any well-lighted room by anyone used to cameras. Second, it permits *immediate re-running*. This gives the speaker a priceless chance to see and hear his presentation from the point of view of his audience. Third, the tape can be erased and re-used.

In a rehearsal a coach and friendly critics can refrain from interrupting during a speaker's run-through and can point out at once details that need improving while the speaker watches the tape being re-run. It can be stopped wherever desired and run over again and discussed. A speaker will not benefit much by watching himself on the monitor as he rehearses. A similar rehearsal in a professional TV studio under the guidance of a professional coach would be superior in certain respects, but it would be much more expensive and often much less convenient.

As portable video-tape recorders come into general use and go through the customary improvements, they should find imaginative uses for special presentations. The most apparent use would seem as a cheap substitute for film—a situation in which someone presents interviews with several authorities in order to help convince a small group that a certain course of action is desirable. Or the presentation by a distinguished visitor to a small group might be repeated later before several other groups.

Demonstrations and Exhibits Make Presentations More Tangible

A neglected aid in oral presentations is the demonstration. Technical persons especially have a weakness for talking *about* materials and products and depending solely on graphs and tables to make their words convincing. What can you say about the strength of a laminate as persuasive as hitting it with a hammer? What can you put on a slide that will prove the heat resistance of a protective coating as well as subjecting it to the flame of a blow torch? How can you bring home to sales trainees what you are trying to tell them as well as by role playing?

Not only are demonstrations effective because they are close to reality. They also add change of pace and dramatic interest.

The chief danger of demonstrations is that they can easily get out of hand. Two possible results are: a) The demonstration may blunt your message—the audience may be entertained without understanding, let us say, how reduction in labor and maintenance costs of a protective coating will offset its high price. b) Passing samples may create undue distraction. The audience should be invited to come up to see samples after a presentation. Samples should be handed around only in talks to a few people.

In rehearsing your use of demonstrations, be sure to check on visibility. Demonstrating something that only the people up in the front of a large room can see makes for a poor presentation. Either the objects used are too small to be seen more than a few feet or the action cannot be seen at all by most of the audience. If your demonstration cannot be seen, you might arrange to have it made into a short film or filmstrip.

You can increase the effectiveness of certain presentations by having an exhibit to go with them. Anyone would consider this self-evident at a trade show where the exhibit is usually the essential part of the presentation. But what might seem to you a straightforward stand-up-and-talk presentation can sometimes be strongly reinforced by an accompanying exhibit.

Some of the elements that would be part of the graphics of a presentation on a certain topic—photographs, diagrams, and basic copy—would probably be part of an exhibit. And some of the things that would be used in a demonstration would also probably be part of an exhibit. In preparing a free-stand, wall, or table exhibit, however, a designer can achieve a special kind of silent communication by means of lighting, color, attractive art, and ingenious effects, such as a mock-up, cutaway model, or working model. If you wish, recordings, sound films, and filmstrips can give the rest of your presentation for you.

Some exhibits are surprisingly expensive to have designed, constructed, transported, installed, and serviced. Yet for occasions where an exhibit can deliver your message beyond the time that you can address your audience—as in recruiting, in training, at an open house, at a stockholders' annual meeting, or during a fund-raising campaign—the gain may justify the expense. Other exhibits can be simple and inexpensive and can be carried in neat folding containers. They can serve as something for you to point to during a presentation or for you to use during a demonstration.

Written Material May Be a Necessary Supplement

Distribution of wads of written material is a sure-fire way to kill a presentation. Your audience, whether 100 or one, reads while you talk and does not pay attention to what you say. Or there is much rustling of paper and whispering, while your listeners try to follow where you are in the text.

But sometimes written material has its place at a presentation.

At a professional society or trade association meeting, for instance, it often helps both you and your audience to have copies of your talk available *after you finish*. Be sure to announce at the opening of your presentation that these copies are available, so that note-taking will not be necessary. Having such material to distribute saves you from having to go into detail any more than your time or audience analysis tells you is desirable.

After a sales or technical call on a customer, you may leave data sheets, reprints, and other written matter.

After a presentation to a management group, you may have a previously prepared summary memorandum ready for those who wish one.

On occasion—especially when you wish to engage in a problem-solving session with a group—it may be wise to distribute written matter beforehand. With time to consider a complex problem or an extensive analysis, your audience will be better prepared to follow your presentation, to accept your recommendations, or to offer thoughtful suggestions. Thus you not only may save time; you may save yourself from having your ideas misunderstood or rejected. This practice is common before meetings of boards of directors.

A presentation may be *about* a piece of writing, such as a budget or an advertising contract. You may have to go through it point by point. Be sure that you have enough copies and that pages and items are clearly marked so that your listeners can follow your presentation without confusion.

If you are going to distribute written matter at a presentation, have it carefully edited and proofread before it is duplicated. Have more than enough copies duplicated and, if desirable, bound in a cover well beforehand. And plan exactly when you will distribute it and how you will use it.

Part III
Making Oral
Presentations

11

Handling Yourself
on Your Feet

Woodrow Wilson wrote in *When a Man Comes to Himself:*

Some actors play with a certain natural passion, an unstudied directness, without grace, without modulation, with no study of the masters or consciousness of the pervading spirit of the plot; others give all their thought to their costume and think only of the audience; a few act as those who have mastered the secrets of a serious art, with deliberate subordination of themselves to the great end and motive of the play, spending themselves like good servants, indulging no wilfulness, obtruding no eccentricity, lending heart and tone and gesture to the perfect progress of the action. These have "found themselves," and have all the ease of a perfect adjustment.

When, as Wilson hoped, you "find yourself," like a great actor you will lend "heart and tone and gesture to the perfect progress" of your oral presentations. You, too, will have "all the ease of a perfect adjustment."

Three Principles Underlie Skilful Oral Presentations

Every skilful oral presentation goes back to three principles:

1) *Full knowledge of your subject and careful preparation of your presentation.* You are involved in a fraudulent operation if you try to get by without both of these assets.

2) *Sensitive adjustment to the audience and to the situation.* Not only be sure to identify your audience as you go along; identify them accurately and courteously. A candidate for the presidency of the United States was once the chief speaker at the annual meeting of his college fraternity. Throughout he referred with deep emotion to the profound influence membership in Phi Theta Delta had had on his life. He evoked mirth instead of applause because the fraternity is Phi Delta Theta.

One of the commonest and least courteous ways of referring to an audience is "you people." The vague generalization has an irritating undertone of condescension. It suggests that the speaker belongs to a superior caste and cannot bother to find out to whom he is speaking.

3) *Awareness of how to make your personality contribute positively.* The person you seem to be has what the psychologists call a *subliminal* effect on your audience. This means that below the threshold of consciousness your audience develop attitudes toward you. By extension, they develop attitudes toward your subject and even the organization you may represent. Especially if they do not know you well, the members of the audience will read the signals you flash at them the moment you mount the rostrum or step into an office. Appearances inevitably count.

Practice can help you apply these three principles more than might seem possible. Instruction under competent teachers can do a great deal. Observation of experienced speakers helps, too. It is nearly impossible for you to imagine what effect you have on other people. Therefore candid criticism both before and after presentations is highly desirable.

Appearing before an audience often has a curious effect on a speaker. A common blunder is for him to try to be somebody he is not. You do not have to do much to tip off the audience that you are not being yourself. A stilted manner of speaking and an unusual choice of words are the usual clues. Unnaturalness quickly sounds like insincerity, especially in a persuasive situation. A moderately skilful speaker who radiates sincerity is more effective than an insincere-sounding spellbinder. Be sincere. Use your natural vocabulary. Be yourself—but your best self.

An inexperienced speaker often confuses his role with that of an after-dinner speaker. The first aim of an after-dinner speaker is to entertain, no matter what it is ostensibly. He is usually paid, sometimes indirectly, according to his success as an entertainer. He may give the same talk 100 times. And the pro invariably works harder at any game than the amateur does.

Your aim in making a presentation is more modest and straightforward than that of an after-dinner speaker. You have no reason to compare yourself with him. Yet like him you should work hard on every presentation, and you should see what you can do to add something extra to make your effort interesting. Not unlikely, much more depends on one of your presentations than on all the after-dinner speeches you will ever be called on to make. So you are a pro, after all. Try to make every presentation as if you believe you are one.

Rehearsals Ensure Good Performances

The world's greatest violinists practice as much as eight hours a day. Broadway stars of long experience rehearse under a director for weeks before a play tries out in Hartford or Harrisburg. Then the performance is changed and rehearsed up to and after the first night on Broadway. To give any kind of public performance without practice and rehearsing is rank amateurism. If your presentations have any genuine significance, you should seek competent help in your rehearsals. Professional paid-for direction is best.

Rehearsing is profitable the more nearly it approaches reality. Observe the following suggestions:

Have your preparation entirely complete before scheduling a rehearsal. Have your talk all organized and your audio-visual aids in final shape to use.

If you are using slides or charts, be sure to mark your manuscript or notes with cues you cannot miss. Since you may under-line other points, draw a box around "Slide 8," or whatever the proper cue is, at the place where you want to be reminded.

Schedule the first rehearsal two weeks before the presentation is to be made.

As near as possible, rehearse in conditions similar to those you expect.

Have present to hear you the persons who can best criticize your material, your audience approach, and your delivery. Tell your trial audience first about your situation and audience anal-ysis together with your controlling purpose. Ask them to criticize in *terms of probable audience reaction—first for subject matter, second for presentation.*

If you are using visual aids, ask your critics to watch for errors, unclear communication, poor visibility, and discrepancies be-tween what they see and what you say.

Write down notes on all suggestions. Ask for amplification, if necessary. Ask all members of the trial audience their reaction to points made. Do not waste time defending yourself. Offer no alibis. Thank your critics for all suggestions and act on those suggestions that seem valid.

If the occasion is to include questions and answers, have your advisers role-play and ask you questions from the various points of view likely to be represented. Receive suggestions on how to improve your question handling.

Have someone time you exactly, though you should have your time worked out before the rehearsal. A stop watch is useful for exact timing and for taking time out for interruptions. During the first rehearsal, particularly, interruptions for suggestions are desirable.

Most important, try like an actor to imagine the real situation. Then do all the things suggested in this book to improve your presentations.

If your rehearsal is poor, you may do better under real condi-tions, but do not count on it. No professional speaker or actor is ever satisfied that he can make a good public appearance until his rehearsals are satisfactory. He has to have his presentation cold, not merely every word but every effect, too.

It is doubly necessary to rehearse if your script or graphics material or both have been prepared by someone else. The disadvantages of using a script have been discussed. The more elevated your position in an organization, the more likely it is that you will sometimes have to rely on prepared material. But the higher you are, the worse it is for you to be fumbling your lines, mispronouncing words, giving inept inflections, and overshooting the ends of sentences.

Under some conditions it may be courteous to acknowledge who prepared some of the material you are using. On the other hand, though it is no disgrace for a busy executive to have someone else write a script for him, especially if he shared in the planning, it is usually poor taste to make any reference publicly to such help. Remarks such as, "That's what it says here" or "Those are the figures they gave me," make the audience lose confidence in the speaker.

The best way to master the ideas and facts in a script prepared by someone else is to read it aloud several times. Then you discover passages that might give you trouble. They may be matters of fact that need checking before you can say them with authority. They may involve ideas that you do not understand and need to discuss with someone before they become your own. Or they may be verbal combinations that do not sound natural when you say them. They have to be put into your own idiom.

This preliminary reading will lead to changes that will make your presentation go much more smoothly. They will, that is, if you make them in time for retyping of the script. Then you can face your audience with a clean copy and not one messed up with interlinear and marginal pencillings impossible to handle fluently. Or, better yet, you may reduce the prepared material to your own notes.

As suggested, tape recording a rehearsal can speed up the improvement of a presentation. You can then put yourself more readily in the place of your audience.

Personal Appearance Is a Matter of Taste— Good Taste

Your personal appearance is always part of your presentation. Any serious presentation deserves the same attention to personal grooming, dress, and manners that you would bestow on a semi-formal social occasion.

For a dance or a dinner you would probably wear a white shirt and tie, have your suit pressed, and shine your shoes. You would shave, get a haircut, if you needed one, and see that your fingernails were presentable. The importance of the impression you make when you give a presentation justifies the same care that you take for a dance or a dinner.

Now and then you read rules about how the well-groomed man should dress and look. Authorities say: Always wear a white shirt to business; never wear a bow tie. Such absolutism suggests a source outside the regular ranks of business, industry, and government, perhaps an advertising agency copy-writer for haberdashery, or a woman's magazine columnist, or the oracle of Delphi.

In reality, since being well groomed is an art, it admits of individual variation in taste. One highly respected board chairman wears a bow tie and a rough-finish custom-made suit every day and always looks well dressed. Different fashions exist in different regions, social groups, and situations. The ten-gallon hat of Dallas and the tweed jacket of Princeton may seem an affectation on Wall Street. If you are a Wall Street broker, you would see no reason for wearing either piece of apparel to a presentation to a client. Yet if you are a native of Dallas or Princeton, you might with propriety wear your native dress to a presentation in a Wall Street board room. If, however, you had reason to believe that you would make a better impression if you dressed less conspicuously, you probably would consider it wise to do so.

Our concern here is only with presentations. In circumstances more extraordinary than probably will be your lot, bizarre dress together with hair and beard as luxuriant as that of the silver gibbon might help along a presentation much better than, say, a Madison Avenue image.

Under normal conditions, a well-groomed appearance is part of a presentation. Your audiences will not make excessive demands on you to conform. The more sophisticated they are, the more they appreciate variations in personal style. Provincial audiences may think care lavished on drape of shoulder, knotting of four-in-hand, and linking of French cuffs to be a form of narcissism. A more worldly audience can tolerate exquisiteness and even deliberate eccentricity much more easily than the crudity of striped ties with checked shirts, unshined shoes with carpenters' toes, breast pocket bristling with writing tools, ostentatious rings and necktie jewelry, and similar evidences of indifference to what is the consensus of good taste among persons with the background of that audience.

Let common sense, observation, good manners, and your wife, together with your audience and situation analysis, be your guide to how you look during your presentations.

Compose Your Thoughts Before You Begin

Once you arrive on the scene of your presentation, you have work to do. If the setting is unfamiliar, study the physical setup. If the occasion is unusually significant, try to visit the room as far ahead as you can. If you are using audio-visual aids, use that fact as an excuse for a careful inspection of the equipment, acoustics, and any special conditions you will face. It is a perilous thing to walk into a room you have not seen before and make a major presentation.

Let us assume that you are making a presentation to a large audience. What can you do as you sit on the platform while other speakers precede you, while other business is being transacted, or even while you are being introduced? At this time the inexperienced speaker often becomes bemused with a sense of his importance. Or like a bridegroom before a wedding he turns numb with foreboding. He does not really come into focus until from out of the buzzing around him he filters the signal to begin, moves to the lectern, and mechanically utters his opening remarks.

Take a leaf out of the book of the experienced speaker. Use the time you have before you stand up to speak to compose your thoughts. Instead of looking at the audience with your mind idling, you often can manage a speeded-up review of your entire presentation. Often you sit in front of your audience through lengthy committee reports and other business and through presentations by one or more other speakers. Use that time.

Without looking at your notes, you can run through the salient points to remember. So as you sit, relaxed but not slouched, you silently coach yourself somewhat in the following manner: The man introducing me is Dr. Garbisch, not Garbage ... I must raise my voice. I've noticed that even with the mike the people in back have been straining to hear ... We're running late. I'll skip that story about the Civil War and do the quick one about the Kentucky colonel ... I must remember not to dally in section 1 ... I'll set my watch to start right on the hour, and I'll stop at the half hour. That will give plenty time for questions and not drag things out ... The figures for employed women are about 25 million or about one-third of the work force....

If you concentrate during these vital minutes, you can visualize the structure of your presentation and remind yourself of passages that require special treatment. You can also put yourself in the right frame of mind. You can tell yourself that you have done your homework. You do have a message. Your audience not only wants to hear it—they need to hear it. Thus, as athletes say, you can be "up" for your presentation when you begin to speak.

Before you get up to speak, study your audience. Do they look alert or apathetic? What is their composition? Are they what you expected? Or do you see a reason for changing part of your presentation? A speaker about a job-training program at a country high school had to change his material on the spot when he found half his audience were adults, women as well as men.

Even one person in the audience may have an effect on what you say. A speaker brought to a Southern city to present suggestions for an adult education center made some hurried changes in his text when he learned that in the audience was a distinguished philosopher from whom he had borrowed some of his ideas. Many a speaker has silently blue-pencilled some of his remarks on discovering a reporter or a woman in the audience. But more subtly, an experienced speaker can estimate the interest level of an audience and decide what he needs to do to hold their attention.

What preceding speakers say may have an effect on what you say. You may be able to get a positive response from the audience by indicating honest concurrence with points made by other speakers. You not only win recognition for fairness and good manners. You also establish awareness of a common interest that you are usually trying to establish by logical evidence.

In addition, preceding speakers will often say things bearing directly on what you propose to say, and you may have to leave something out, use different material, answer questions, or disprove statements made. Failing to listen to them may make you look obtuse. Do not, however, in acknowledging what others have said, be drawn away from your planned presentation to the extent of wrecking your time schedule or muddling your purpose and organization.

Poise and Enthusiasm Please an Audience

When you stand up to make a presentation, whether among your daily associates or before a roomful of strangers, think of your own reactions as you sit in the audience listening to any speaker. Do you not wish him well?—not altogether out of charity, but also because you do not care to be subjected to an exhibition of nervousness or ineptness. Such an exhibition makes you uncomfortable. Discomfort easily turns to rejection, as in the unsympathetic attitude of one child toward another who is crying.

The two standard physical types in unsatisfactory presentations are: a) a fidgety body and a tense voice, and b) a slumping body and a monotonous voice. The self-conscious or inept speaker twists and shuffles. He grimaces. He chokes up and mangles his sentences. He stands on one foot, thrusts one shoulder forward, and imitates a corkscrew. Tall or short, he makes himself little by draping himself over the lectern, table, or handy chair back. Sometimes his feet shuffle, while he sways his torso like a sailor on a rolling deck. Sometimes he stands rigid, his face dull, his voice flat, like an eighth-grader reciting Shakespeare, without feeling for the subject or the audience.

What is your attitude toward such a speaker? You feel that he is being discourteous toward you. You have granted him time to present his case, often time that you would prefer to spend otherwise. You should not have to put up with his unreadiness or his distaste for the job he has chosen to do. How do you respond? By downgrading the case he presents to the level of his competence in presenting it.

A variant of the incompetent speaker is the one who knows his subject but who looks and sounds tired or bored. What is your attitude toward him? You think, if your material does not interest you enough to make you *seem* interested, why inflict it on me? Professors and readers of technical and professional papers often affect this lack of enthusiasm. This affectation is more irritating than the gaucherie of the unprepared. Because it betrays an underlying smugness, after the first few sentences you probably cast charity and fair-mindedness aside and wickedly amuse yourself pouncing on errors of fact and thinking up contrary lines of reasoning. No one making chips-down presentations can risk this kind of response.

Turn the question around. What sort of speaker do you like to hear? What sort do you tend to give your support to before he has made more than a start on his presentation? Is it not the speaker who seems to have all of his muscles under control and seems alive, alert? Do you not prefer the voice that is animated and resonant? This combination of control and dynamism, both in action and in voice, is something that we popularly associate with success. This is ingenuous, for success is a noun that can be used to tag many different kinds of achievement, some of which have nothing to do with our subject. Within our observable experience, however, men who have followed rigorous disciplines —surgery, the sea, or politics—and who have done something notable as leaders of others, do tend to attain a certain radiant equilibrium, a fusion of poise and enthusiasm.

You may in modesty protest that you do not aspire so high. Yet have you not felt the same sense of equilibrium in the presence of quite humble people? A sense that they are at peace with themselves, glad to breathe and move, fascinated by whatever they are doing, whether keeping bees or fighting fires, and certain of your good will and interest in their work.

There is no easy way for you to reach this state of vitality and control. It is, of course, a result of your whole way of life, your upbringing, your education, your work, your health, and your emotional make-up. But you have two reasons to be hopeful that you can do something about this important aspect of your presentations without insincerity. The first is that actors, even amateur actors, manage to achieve such a presence by first imagining what it will take to project a positive personality across the footlights and then rehearsing until they do. The second is the report of history and your own experience—the evidence, trite but incontrovertible, that the persons who have become great platform presences have many times started with much greater handicaps than you have. The only difference may be in the will to succeed.

The young men who are today running the mile under four minutes have exactly the same equipment that runners had fifty years ago when the four-minute mile was a mirage. They have added vision and intelligent coaching to will.

If you have the will to excel in your presentations, you will strive for the muscular control, alert attention, vibrant interest in subject, eagerness to communicate, and quiet assurance that all effective speakers have. If you cultivate the manifestations that embody these qualities—through conscious practice and perhaps through amateur drama—in time they will become part of you. Then through your poise and enthusiasm you will command the respect of your audiences.

Keep Direct Contact with Your Audience

The gestures of old-fashioned oratory are no longer in vogue. Many speakers, however, use distracting gestures. They rub their nose, twiddle a pencil, and flip their hand as though throwing something away. Or else they turn rigid by getting an armlock on themselves behind their back or a wristlock in front. Others jingle coins or keys.

Gestures that grow naturally out of the thought and do not lag behind it are effective. Mechanical arm pumping or finger waggling looks self-conscious and often comic. If you are going to use gestures, do so without thinking. If you have to think about them by the time you make an actual presentation, they are bound to come a split second after the thought and be a liability, not an asset.

Sometimes a speaker concentrates so hard on what he is saying that his face turns wooden. A smile, a raising of the eyebrows, a nod of the head—these can be far more expressive gestures than the pumphandle kind. They come more naturally as a part of the act of communication. Or they do if the speaker is aware of what he is saying and is not just remembering words.

If you have to point at anything on a chart or screen, do so firmly, exactly, and briefly. Use a pointer, not your arm alone. You can get a collapsible pointer to carry, and you can use a special flashlight for pointing out details on screens. Do not distract the audience by waving your pointer all over the place or by dragging it over the surface of the graphics as you talk.

No matter what the circumstances may be, look your audience in the eye. In an auditorium this means that you turn your head and look at specific persons in different parts of the room. Do not fasten your gaze on your notes, on your chart or screen, or on a point above the heads of your listeners. Maintain eye contact. Talk with your eyes.

If you are using a chart or screen, do not stand looking at it with your back to half the audience. Let it speak for itself. Your job is talking to the audience. A glance once in a while at your graphics should suffice to steer you, if you know what you are talking about. Pointing occasionally to a significant detail is desirable. Turning every minute or so to stare at graphics when they offer nothing new to read suggests a desire to run away from your audience. Face the audience most of the time. Particularly be sure to include in your gaze any part of the audience that may be somewhat out of range at the side of the room or in a gallery.

When you are using notes, hold them in your hand and bring them up to your eye level when you glance at them. Do not put your notes on a table and then emulate a heron spearing fish in a pond. If you are talking at a lectern, direct your eyes and your voice over the top of it. Do not put your notes on it and fasten your eyes on them, so that your voice bounces off instead of going out to the audience. Some lecterns are adjustable up and down, a boon if you are short or tall.

When you have a number of sheets of paper to deal with in an oral presentation, a looseleaf ring notebook is desirable. Loose sheets can easily become mixed, with awkward results. If they are stapled into a notebook, you often need both hands to keep the pages open. With a looseleaf ring notebook you can flip the sheets with one hand, and they will lie flat. For most talks a small-ring notebook is more appropriate than the usual size.

You Can Learn to Use Your Voice More Effectively

Your voice is the chief instrument of your oral presentations. Yet how much attention have you ever given it? How much attention has anyone you know ever given his voice? Once more ask yourself whether your presentations or your golf game—or whatever your hobby may be—is more important to you. Then you may decide that your voice deserves a lot more cultivating than it has had.

If you are serious in heeding this suggestion, then you should go to a university speech department and have your voice analyzed. You can count on a university to be thorough, dependable, and reasonable in fee. You cannot count on independent voice teachers in any of these respects. Many are competent and ethical, but it is not easy to find out who they are. The analysis of your voice should include what to do to improve your way of using it. This may involve voice classes for a year or more, or private lessons. It will certainly involve having you learn more about using your voice and taking steps to correct specific weaknesses.

Though you should have professional help, you should also listen to yourself on tape recordings and re-do passages that seem not up to the standard you think yourself capable of reaching. Here are five areas on which to concentrate.

Breathing. The first requirement in developing a good voice for oral presentations is to acquire voice control. Breathe fully while you talk, and speak in natural breath groups—that is, inhale and exhale without strain while you are speaking. If your voice becomes hoarse or strained, you are not using it correctly. Regular breathing is necessary also to give your voice full volume. Under normal conditions an experienced speaker can project his voice strongly for hours without tiring.

Enunciation. Next, you have to open your mouth and use your lips to make your enunciation effective. To keep from mumbling and slurring and to make your voice carry in a large room, you have to have plenty of jaw and lip action. The way to develop it is to exaggerate when you are rehearsing. Reading aloud to your wife or children is a good way of practicing.

Modulation. A good speaking voice is more than clear; it is well modulated. It is not harsh or nasal. It has a pleasing melody.

Naturalness. Use your voice to talk to your audience, not to harangue them or bore them. Try above everything for natural stressing. Avoid the jerkiness that comes from pauses at unnatural places, as "I went—to the—store."

A great many speakers fall into a habit of artificial accenting. The result is a monotonous rhythm. The commonest pattern is to start sentence after sentence with energy and clarity and then to run down until the end is swallowed and almost inaudible. Almost as common is the trick of mechanically underscoring the key word in every phrase without reference to relative significance.

Variety. To hold your audience, you need variety, the same variety that is in your thought. In natural speech you talk slower and faster, softer and louder, according to your thought and feeling. Some words and sentences have only incidental value and can be "thrown away"—that is, disposed of quickly and without emphasis. A key sentence may require emphasis on almost every word, or it may be repeated to drive it home. You can give the audience a sense of the importance of what you are saying by lowering your voice or talking deliberately, as well as by hammering your points.

Variety in phrasing and emphasis is necessary to help communication. If your voice reflects the flow of the thought and the relative importance of parts of your talk, you are aiding the audience to comprehend. Keep in mind that in all communication you are answering unspoken questions—What are you talking about? What are the main points? What does that mean? What are you talking about at this stage? Why is this point especially important? For example? What comes next?

Every speaker has some undesirable speech habit. Winston Churchill's vowels suffered a nasal cockney taint, and Franklin Delano Roosevelt used to say, "My fellow Amurricans!" Most of the rest of our presidents have spoken regional dialects, often in ways far from appealing to other regions. You probably have one or two regionalisms or other negative speech habits that your colleagues will point out to you, if you ask.

The "uh" habit is as prevalent and unpopular with audiences as the common cold. For mysterious reasons, girls now substitute "ummm" for "uh." "Well" at the opening of sentence after sentence is high on the list of boring crutch words. Many of us have idiosyncrasies all our own. One otherwise excellent speaker says "mawdren" for modern; another says "I mean" and "you know" parenthetically dozens of times in every talk; another uses the clumsy locution "as far as something or other is concerned" with tiresome frequency. But the most common speech weakness is lack of expression—a flat, dull, unresonant, unenthusiastic voice.

If you must clear your throat, take time to do so, and do it quietly and away from a microphone.

The best ways to improve your speech are: a) Listen to it on a tape recorder. b) Ask competent critics for suggestions. c) Pay close attention to the speech of the best radio and television commentators. d) Pay for professional coaching.

Your Opening Remarks Must Do Several Things

If circumstances make the use of a microphone desirable, use it. Do not fight the mike. Inexperienced speakers often say, "I don't need that thing!" They are then unheard beyond the third row, or the audience has to strain to hear them. Acoustics can be tricky. Relatively small rooms can be "dead." Large rooms often have dead areas in them. The extra volume a microphone gives amplifies the authority of the speaker. It enables him to dominate an audience when his natural voice might not permit him to do so.

If you use a microphone, be sure that you adjust it to your height. The proper height is one that allows you to stand firmly on your feet and look at the audience without worrying about the microphone at all. The microphone should be level with your mouth as your eyes engage the audience.

If you are wearing a necklace type of microphone, be sure that it is high enough so that it catches your voice satisfactorily. Holding it in your hand may give you better reception.

Test the microphone in advance of your presentation, if you possibly can.

If the microphone malfunctions during your talk, stop and ask for adjustments. If these cannot be made quickly, abandon the microphone. Do not try to talk above the squeals of a defective PA system. Of course, you might learn how to make adjustments yourself.

If you are speaking at a stand, keep your weight squarely on both feet. Do not clutch the stand or drape yourself over it. Do not skate.

Do not start talking before you get in position, especially if you are using a microphone. Do not mumble and stumble. Do not turn and say things to the chairman as you are shuffling papers. Look into the eyes of specific members of the audience, no matter how small or large it is.

As you are about to utter your first words, do three things to get voice control: a) *Swallow.* b) *Take a deep breath.* c) *Speak in a voice that you are sure everyone will hear.* Your voice should be loud and resonant, not strangled or muffled. It should be crisp and decisive, not faltering and apologetic.

Do not talk about yourself or your lack of speech-making accomplishments. This false modesty calls attention to you, is not flattering to the audience, and starts you off with a strike. Self-consciousness is a form of vanity. It indicates that you are more concerned about yourself than about your message.

Your listeners are interested in themselves, not you. They are interested in what they can get from your talk. Above all, they are *not* interested in your troubles, true or imaginary, in preparing for the occasion. Never admit that you have rehearsed or that you have given the same talk to another audience. *Never apologize* about anything, except as good manners require you to do so— as for lateness—and then convincingly but briefly.

As previously indicated, your opening should be planned on a basis of your audience and situation analysis. Occasionally, before you are called on, you can pick up something that has been said by a previous speaker and use it as an effective bridge to your own talk. "I am glad to hear Mr. Robinson discuss costs in his talk because I am going to discuss savings through better planning."

Planned or impromptu, your opening remarks usually do four things:

1. *Command the attention of your listeners.* This you may do by standing silent and looking at them. This undoubtedly is the most effective way. It is fatal to start to talk, especially in a voice that is below the level necessary to be heard throughout a room, before all of the audience is seated or listening. It is even desirable on occasion to throw away a line or two, even when the audience is listening—maybe, "On the way in from the airport the cab-driver was telling me what a fine plant you have here." This brief stalling brings them into focus for the more vital material.

2. *Establish your attitude.* Much of the time this involves no thought or skill. Other times it is of the utmost importance. Let us say that your situation analysis tells you that you may expect some antagonism. Both what you say and your manner, therefore, at the outset should be disarming and reassuring. You might indicate sincere regret for something that has gone wrong, guarantee the satisfactory outcome of a problem, or offer a reminder of common interests and pleasant mutual experiences. Such initial statements combined with *a calm and friendly manner* can do a great deal to establish the proper tone at the beginning of the talk. Defensiveness, apparent indifference to what the audience may be thinking, signs of tension or belligerence—such attitudes can lick you before you begin.

3. *Identify your audience.* Show that you know who they are, what their interests are, and how much you respect them. This may be no more elaborate than expressing your pleasure at having

the opportunity to explain polymer chemistry to the Bullock Creek P.T.A. Even then you might get your come-uppance if you have not taken the trouble to find out that in the audience is someone who is well acquainted with your subject. In such a case, you might adopt a modest demeanor and from time to time inject remarks such as, "Would you say that is so, Dr. Silane?"

4. *Make clear what your controlling purpose is.* A great deal of misunderstanding occurs in many speech situations because the audience believes the speaker is trying to do something other than what he has in mind. The trouble is often just that he keeps it in mind. For instance, a statement like, "I have come to hear your complaints and to straighten out whatever difficulties you are having," might head off considerable emotionalism.

Your audience analysis should uncover any fears your audience may have about what you *might* say. If your listeners have any grounds for believing that you might be bringing bad news, they will often listen so hard for it that they do not hear anything else you say. Keep in mind at all times that you are answering unspoken questions.

12

Managing the

Oral Presentation

In the previous chapter we talked about how you handled yourself during an oral presentation. Now let us consider how you manage your material during the presentation. Thorough preparation, we have been stressing, is your best assurance that your material will satisfactorily fall within the three critical parameters—your purpose, the desires of the audience, and the specifics of the situation. Yet once you are on your feet, you still have to be alert about what you do with what you have planned to say.

Make Your Purpose Plainly Evident

Sometimes, even after elaborate preparation, a speaker is lulled into thinking that because his organization is logically clear, his audience cannot fail to follow it. This is a rash assumption. The main justification of an oral presentation over a written one is precisely that you can stress and adjust your material until the purpose and pattern do emerge. In a written presentation key concepts are wrapped up in a single sentence—often in a single word—and they may float by without being separated from other

153

concepts of less importance. The same danger exists in an oral presentation when your material is so familiar to you that your very fluency interferes with communication.

So, once your opening remarks are out of the way, you move warily into your prepared material. Here is where looking into the eyes of your audience can save you from rushing by a key concept. Something like this may take place: You are an executive from a Pennsylvania chemical company that has just announced plans to build a large plant near a Tennessee river town. You are addressing a meeting of the leading citizens. Your purpose is to convince them that your company will respect its community obligations. You particularly seek to reassure them that waste from the plant will not pollute the river.

Your planned presentation calls first for a section on the story of your company and then a second on the operations of the new plant. By the time you finish your introductory pleasantries, however, you have observed that the only smiling faces in the audience belong to the businessmen who have had a hand in the preliminary transactions. The rest of the audience remains glum. You realize that by the time you get to your assurances, the fears of this group may have hardened into hostility. You shift your plan and say: "I am happy to assure you that your river will not be polluted—your drinking water will not be contaminated—your children can continue to swim in the river—the fishing will be just as good as it has always been. My company has spent a million dollars on our waste disposal system. Let me explain how it works."

In this example you would be making your purpose stand out and relating it to the interests of the audience in the opening minute. You would of course thread your reassurances throughout the talk, and you would offer evidence in a variety of forms to prove the trustworthiness of your statements.

Rhetoric, Gestures, and Voice
Keep Your Pattern Clear

Keeping the pattern of the presentation clear at all times must, as we have been saying, begin with a clear 1-2-3 organization in the first place. But that will not carry you through an oral presentation by itself. You have to be ever alert for the opportunity to reinforce the logic of organization by the manner of your treatment. Failure to do this is probably the most common weakness in otherwise excellent presentations. Yet, if when you are through, your audience cannot sum up what you have said, have you not failed?

Apart from your audio-visual aids, you bring out the pattern of your presentation by rhetorical devices, by gestures, and by how you use your voice. The most useful rhetorical devices are repetition, restatement, and pointing and stressing words and phrases. As you say, "I am happy to assure you that your river will not be polluted," you may realize that some of the audience show signs of not realizing what you have said. You may then say, "Let me say that again," and repeat it. Or you may restate the same idea by saying, "Yes, the water in your river will be just as pure when our plant goes on stream as it is now." "Let me say that again" is a typical phrase for pointing out to the audience what they should note about what you are saying.

A gesture that will help establish the basic pattern of your presentation in the mind of your audience has to be noticeable. Merely sawing the air as you go from one main section of your talk to another is probably not enough. You might gesture with your whole body. How? By standing quietly and allowing time for the audience to think back over the section you have just completed. By walking to another spot on the platform or otherwise changing your position in relation to the audience. By taking your time in changing a chart. By presenting graphics for the new section and silently studying them along with the audience for several moments. By changing your expression and even your muscular reaction as your mind enters into consideration of the new material. In some such way you signal the audience that a major transition is taking place, and they relax a little and then get ready for what comes next.

Your voice is a musical instrument. With it you can play all sorts of tunes. You can lower it and make it say—what comes next is something confidential I am sharing with you. You can raise it and make it say—now comes something still more important. You can make it calm and confident, and it will say—so much for what has gone before, now comes something that you will like even better.

Few details in the management of an oral presentation are more important than keeping the audience aware of what the major sections are and when you are shifting from one to another.

Be the Master of Your Audio-Visual Aids

Be sure your audio-visual aids are suitable to your material. For instance, do not use slides that require a darkened room for a few sets of figures that can easily be put on a chart. Do not ask a group to struggle through pages of figures in a mimeographed report if you wish merely to tell them about a few highlights. Do not prepare a large number of charts to represent single key words in your talk. Then you have to direct the attention of the audience away from yourself while you keep busy changing sheets.

Be sure the charts, projection screen, demonstration table, or other aids are not so placed that they drag you away from the only microphone and keep changing your voice from full volume to a thin piping. Do not come between the audience and your charts or other aids. Work from the side, not the front, and do not turn your back to the audience.

If you have something to demonstrate, be sure that it is large enough to be seen by everyone in the room. Hold it high enough to be seen by all. Or if it has to lie on a table, do not come between it and the audience.

Remember that the members of the audience on the sides of an auditorium are just as important as the members in the center.

If you are going to operate a model or demonstrate something, do it skilfully. Make certain that whatever you say will work, does work. If you are using projection equipment, be sure that you can get the image in the right place without a lot of experimenting.

Sometimes because of necessity or the nature of your film or slides, you will project in complete darkness. You must then be able to talk without notes, or you must have a light at your lectern. Be sure that the lectern light is turned on before the room lights go off and that it does not shine into the eyes of the audience.

A presentation based on slides has a tendency to fall into a too-regular rhythm. To avoid monotony, dispose of some slides more quickly than others.

In a pinch you should always be able to give your presentation without audio-visual aids. Your charts might not be finished on time, your aids might go astray in transit, or a projector might fail. The audience will not be interested in your mishaps. You must be ready with only a word of explanation to go ahead with your talk. Notes on a set of 3 x 5 cards that you can carry with you are always good insurance. You cannot be absolutely sure that your charts, slides, or other aids will be where you want them when you want them or that they will fit local conditions.

Public address systems are notoriously unreliable. The same electrical equipment companies that can be depended upon to send a man to the moon have yet to devise a dependable public address system. Wherever possible, insist on having a trained technician monitor the equipment while you are making your presentation.

Now suppose that what happens all too frequently, does happen—the public address system goes dead or is taken over by gremlins. If speaking is part of your bread and butter existence, you should be able to fill any ordinary auditorium with your natural voice. You should be able to "throw" your voice to the back seats or the gallery without going hoarse in a few minutes. Can you? You can with instruction and practice.

Improvising Is the Acid Test

You are not really a pro at giving a presentation unless you can improvise—adjust your talk as you go along. Here is where having maintained eye contact with your audience pays off. If you see their eyes wavering, a puzzled expression on their faces, a covert exchange of disbelieving looks, or a surreptitious consulting of watches, you know you will have to counter-punch.

The commonest adjustment of all is the painful decision to

cut out some of your material. Often you do not cut it; you summarize it so that the whole presentation hangs together. Often
you can show a chart or slide and sum it up without itemizing.
The audience can pick up the essential information at a glance.

The more difficult midstream adjustment is to introduce new
ideas. This is necessary when you see that your talk is not getting
across. Perhaps you will have to simplify, repeat, restate in different words, or reinforce with additional examples or arguments.
If you are not master of your subject, only of words, you cannot
make this sort of shift smoothly. Then you are in trouble.

If you have to cut or abridge, you had better skip technical
data, examples, refinements of thought rather than hurry your
summary. But *be sure you recap your controlling purpose and
the main points* clearly and emphatically.

On the other hand, improvising is an insidious hazard even for
the well-prepared speaker. Feeling how well he is doing, he suc-
cumbs to the temptation to show off a bit and starts ad libbing.
Such improvising may stop the movement forward, spoil the
tempo, and ruin the overall timing of an otherwise well-planned
presentation. The Latin *ad libitum* means *at one's pleasure.* Ad
libbing often shows that the speaker is taking more pleasure in
indulging his own whims than he is in carrying out his assignment.

Inexpert improvising also comes about when the speaker loses
his hold on his material and starts repeating himself or elabo-
rating what is already clear. Sometimes these unplanned ex-
tensions arise out of panic. Random ideas pop into his head, and
he is not disciplined enough to resist uttering them.

Thorough rehearsals precisely timed and, preferably, tape-
recorded and analyzed, are the best safeguard against loose-
lipped ad libbing.

Control Your Tempo

Setting the right tempo and maintaining it are two important
parts of your presentation. Many of us habitually talk too fast or
too slow when we face an audience. Technical men are often so

familiar with their material that they rattle along at a pace an audience cannot follow unless it is also made up of technical people. Others drag along. Change the pace in order to hold attention. In the main your tempo should be brisk and your tone serious, a reflection of your attitude toward the matter in hand and your appreciation of the opportunity you have to present it.

Humor that comes naturally out of the material is an excellent device for changing the tempo. An unexpected laugh allows the listener to relax his mental grip on the subject. Then he takes a new hold.

The simplest change of tempo is the pause. The pause that follows a rhetorical question—"Now, what do you think we should do next?"—and the pause that follows the completion of a major section of the thought are especially effective.

If you are using charts, consider what happens to your tempo when you interrupt yourself every few minutes to turn your back on the audience and give your attention to the chart. If you have to change sheets, do so quickly and, as far as possible, while facing the audience. Often it is better to have an assistant to do this for you. No able pianist lets his music stop while he turns a page. The tempo of a talk can be just as important as any other feature.

Watch out for "second-half slowdown." In presentations lasting over half an hour the non-professional speaker more often than not finds his voice tiring. He slows his tempo, hits a monotone, and loses his punch. Learn to pace yourself in rehearsals. To get up and give a presentation without several complete rehearsals is like entering a mile run after practicing a few sprints. If you find yourself running out of gas toward the end of a talk, shift to your planned summary end.

Humor and Other Tonal Effects
Influence Audience Reactions

The success of any presentation depends to a considerable degree on its pervasive tone. Without putting their feelings into words, at the end of one of your presentations members of an audience will have a general feeling—that the subject is important, urgent, dull, fascinating—that you are sincere, conceited, optimistic, shrewd, defensive, arrogant, open-minded—or something of the sort. Partly this reaction derives from what you say, but much of it comes from how you say it and how you look and act as you say it.

Much of this response by an audience is, as we have said before, subliminal. Much of it is a reaction to aspects of your personality over which you have no control. But you do have control over much of the tone of every presentation you make. Take humor, for instance. How much humor contributes to presentations is not subject to generalization. Presentations are generally serious affairs. You are not likely to contribute much to the awarding of a contract by telling a funny story to a city council. But if the story is appropriate to the occasion and if you tell it spontaneously, you may relax tension and create a friendlier reception for your case. If the story is not apt or not in good taste, or if you tell it clumsily or as part of an "act," you may help the council to decide against you.

Speakers who go about giving the same talk over and over often fall into the habit of telling several jokes to start with and then following with a joke every few minutes. For speakers with exhibitionist tendencies and for occasions where entertainment, or mere arousing of interest, is the chief goal, this calculated outpouring of humor may be justified. It is hardly a suitable model for the average executive who does not aspire to being regarded as a comedian.

A bit of humor arising spontaneously from the incidents of the moment suggests that you are friendly and unassuming. It gives the audience a quick relaxing of attention without destroying the flow of your presentation. Five points you must watch, however. Your humor should not be personal, unless it is directed at yourself. It should not be sarcastic, even if impersonal. You should not indulge in private jokes that exclude most of the audience. You should not use irony—saying the opposite of what you mean—because you are sure to be misunderstood. And remember to smile as you utter your passing witticism. If you do not smile, some of your audience may think you did not intend to be funny and those who know you did may stifle their laughter.

Audience Participation Enlivens a Presentation

A presentation becomes much more effective if the audience gets into the act. It is not always possible or appropriate for you to put this axiom into use, but you should not forget it. The psychological truth of the value of participation in learning and persuasion is well established: a) You learn more by doing than by merely listening. You learn to play golf by playing. b) You feel a more positive commitment toward something in which you are involved. The good salesman says, "Just try this coat on, sir"; "Here, Mrs. Doakes, feel how easy it is to operate this vacuum cleaner." The fund raiser sees to it that the leading citizens are on the campaign committee.

Audience participation, therefore, may involve nothing more complicated than asking a customer to try on a coat. In some circumstances, especially in a training program, it may involve role-playing. Sales calls on purchasing agents are often simulated behind one-way glass where the audience can observe, but the role-players cannot see out.

The most usual form of audience participation in a presentation is the opportunity to ask questions and to offer comments.

Imaginative use of audience participation can sometimes make the difference between a dull presentation and a lively, memorable one. All magicians, carnies, and evangelists rely heavily on audience participation.

When actual audience participation is impossible or inappropriate, you can also simulate it by devices such as rhetorical questions—"How could you use this machine in your plant?" "What would you do in this situation?" Or simply by saying, "Now think about this next problem."

An Associate in the Audience Can Be Helpful

The visibility and audibility of your presentation must be in terms of the farthest members of your audience. Like the boys at Bunker Hill, when you are far from some of your audience, watch the whites of their eyes. If you see none, the people in the back rows have probably given up on you and gone to sleep.

In planning a presentation, especially for a large room, you may sometimes plant an associate in the back row to signal to you how you are getting over. Here are some signals that you might get used to in rehearsals. Then you can catch them without distraction during an actual presentation:

Finger pointed to lips—*Keep your mouth closer to mike.*
Hand behind ear—*Louder.*
Finger on lips—*Softer.*
Finger pointing to eye—*Look at your audience.*
Circular motion of hand—*Speed it up.*
Hand up, palm out—*Slow down.*
Both hands palm down, pressing downward—*Stand still.*
Wristwatch held up, fingers indicating number of minutes left.
Fingers making a cross—*Thirty seconds left.*
Scissor-like movement of fingers—*Cut some of your material.*
Hand drawn across throat—*Stop.*

Watch your associate in the audience for signals. He may save you from disaster.

If any untoward incident occurs, such as noise in an adjacent room, your associate should act swiftly to take care of it. Many after-lunch and after-dinner speeches are ruined by the merriment of a class reunion in the next room or the crash of dishes in the kitchen. Or you may have need for an object in another room. You will be more comfortable, if you have someone ready to take care of any problem that comes up. Even if you are speaking before a strange audience, you will usually be able to solicit the good offices of someone—not someone who has to be on a platform with you—for this service.

Make the Most of the Question Period

Planning should anticipate the most logical questions that a particular audience would ask about your subject. Sometimes, however, it is advisable to leave a few points unanswered deliberately. Then they get the special attention of being brought up from the floor. If anyone asks a pertinent question you cannot answer satisfactorily, you have not done your homework. Of course, a straightforward "I don't know" can be a satisfactory answer. Otherwise, you will do well to say: "I hadn't thought of that. I'll find out and let you know."

In answering questions, observe three rules: a) *Receive all questions cordially.* b) *Repeat the question* and give the questioner time to change the wording. Then both you and the audience will be clear about what is being asked. Speakers often look foolish because they plunge in to answer questions they misunderstand. c) *Answer briefly.* Few things bore an audience more than an elaborate answer to some side-issue question when they either wish to ask more relevant questions or to go somewhere else.

If the answer to a question will take too long, suggest to the questioner that he see you after the meeting.

If you are offered suggestions that either you have not thought about or that you believe not useful, accept them courteously. "That's an interesting suggestion. I'll look into it" is much better than a churlish "Well, I don't know about that..." or blank silence. In certain circumstances, of course, the courteous thing is to explain why a suggestion will not work. You can still say "thank you" and make the person who made the suggestion feel that he has been constructive.

Questions and comments from the floor sometimes sound hostile when they are not. They merely reflect the self-consciousness of being conspicuous. A person's voice and words may also reflect his being ill at ease because he is speaking from a seated position or from a broad-jumping posture. Sometimes an apparently negative question or comment is offered good humoredly to see what you will say—possibly even to give you a chance to score a point. Do not be ruffled by negative remarks. Your audience will be on your side as long as you remain courteous and agreeable.

Answer foolish questions courteously, without comment. You do not have to suffer fools gladly, but you must suffer them without condescension.

Be on guard for trap questions that lead to answers that compromise you in relation to what you said earlier. When you do not understand the purpose of a question from the floor, ask the questioner politely to explain why he is asking it. Your answer can be much more illuminating if you know whether it is a question that just popped into his head or whether he has a specific problem to which his question is not really the key. If he meant to embarrass you, your question may put him on the defensive to such an extent that he will withdraw his or tone it down.

The question-and-answer period has two important values: a) It provides feedback. It checks your effectiveness. You often discover points your audience misunderstood or points you neglected to cover. b) It provides an excuse for restating and emphasizing key ideas. Never have so much to say that you deny the audience the chance to ask questions. This period is the most profitable and enjoyable part of many meetings, both for the audience and for the speaker.

Feedback is an essential part of improvement in all learning. If you are going to improve your oral presentations, you have to find out how your efforts seem to critical observers. One or more of the persons who offer suggestions during a rehearsal are often on hand at the presentation. As soon as you have a chance, go over their reactions to the content of your talk, your use of audio-visual aids, your voice and posture, and any other observations they have made. Just listen. Do not alibi. Try to learn what you did well, as well as what you did poorly. Often these criticisms can be more enlightening than any others that you ever get. If you cannot pay attention right after a presentation, schedule a review the next day. If you neglect this sort of feedback, you miss a valuable chance to improve your presentations.

13

Dealing with Small

Groups

Some of your most important presentations will take place before small groups, sometimes with an audience of one. Project reviews to management, civic committee reports, calls on customers, task groups to solve problems, and oral reports to supervisors are common small-group presentations.

Rarely can you estimate the consequences of a presentation before a large group. But the consequences of a presentation to one person or to a small group generally can be calculated in terms of attitudes and decisions. Since the attitudes and decision-making of a small group often have much immediate importance for you, it is even more desirable that you plan and rehearse small-group presentations than any other. Think about this. Is it not true that you should take pains in proportion to the significance of the outcome of your presentations, not the size of the audience? Do you?

The Atmosphere of Small Groups Creates Problems

Most of the earlier suggestions for preparing and giving oral presentations apply to presentations before small groups. The atmosphere, however, creates problems that require special treatment.

One of the common situations is that in which you make presentations in an advisory role. You may act in this capacity habitually. Only you may not have thought of going in to talk to your boss or to a management committee or writing a critical memorandum to them as being a presentation. It is. Possibly if you take pains commensurate with the importance of some of the matters you are asked to present, you can better your future prospects.

Failure to think in proper presentation terms may arise from too much back-and-forth familiarity. The informality of an invitation such as "Let's go over the budget after lunch" may throw you off guard. In this instance you might analyze a many-paged budget by highlighting it first on a few charts or slides. You might give a crisp review of the overall picture and then list the critical problems in each major budget area. Instead, what usually happens in these circumstances? The presentation is unplanned and crawls over the figures for hours like a snail exploring a lettuce patch.

The informal atmosphere of a small group may set the tone of a presentation at the conversational level. Your boss, the customer, the committee, or whoever the audience may be tend to treat you as a close colleague, as a guest, or possibly as an unwelcome interruption.

If you do not watch out, the opening remarks may dissolve into something like this: "Ah, yes, Beardsley, you wanted to talk about that idea of yours to expand the museum into a cultural center. I've been thinking about that. Great idea, and I'll tell you how we ought to handle it. What we need here in Wheat City is a place for trade shows. Now I suggest that we cut down that grove of oak trees next to the museum ..." Soon you are listening to a presentation instead of giving one. Or you start your presentation and someone, cutting in as though swapping stories at a luncheon club, says, "You should see what they've done in Minneapolis ..."

After he has made a five-minute contribution, someone else feels constrained to give a critique of the architecture of the Lincoln Center in New York. You sit.

Sometimes the atmosphere of a small group presentation is not informal enough for what you want to accomplish. Therefore you deliberately encourage response from those present, to be sure you have everyone with you. You watch faces for signs of doubt or disbelief. It is your fault if someone misses a turn and is lost in the underbrush from there on. Or if someone sits nursing what he thinks is a devastating criticism that you could have disposed of a half hour earlier. Or if you learn later about opposition that you never knew was present, because you made no effort to smoke it out. Do not think all who are present agree with you because they do not disagree or are personally agreeable toward you.

In a small group you can deal with individual circumstances. In the cultural center illustration, for instance, you might convert the talk about the good things of Minneapolis into endorsement of similar efforts in Wheat City and the discourse about the Lincoln Center into recommendations about the buildings for a local cultural center.

You normally would not appear before a group of twenty or more persons without being expected to make a more or less uninterrupted presentation. But with smaller groups, especially under ten, your goal is to get predetermined results, not to make a formal presentation. Results may be better attained by involving the members of the group in the matter under consideration than by having them listen without interruption to your presentation.

There are times when you must take charge. The best time to start is before you appear. You can arrange in advance that you will have fifteen minutes, or whatever you need, to make your presentation. Here is one time when the word "presentation" conveys explicit meaning. Your audience knows that you mean to do the talking at first. You may have to make this clear after you arrive. You do not issue orders. You say firmly with a smile something like: "Gentlemen, I believe it will save your time if you permit me to take fifteen minutes to present the main features of my plan for a cultural center. Then we can explore the details together."

You generally have a much easier time controlling a small group if you stand up. If the group consists of only one or two, this posture is not natural to assume or to hold. When you do think it desirable to stand, appropriate and interesting graphics will help. Then, though you may not use them much, you have an excuse to stand up in front of even one person—and keep standing. If someone starts a side discussion, you can be silent and look polite but ready to go on to the next point.

If you were presenting a plan for a cultural center, for instance, such aids as an architect's plans and renderings, photographs of existing centers, and financial estimates would justify your standing and continuing to speak until you had finished what you had planned to present. This would be acceptable even with an audience of one.

Personalities Count More in Small Groups

Presentations to small groups mean that your audience analysis must be much more overt. The composition of the group has much more bearing on the success of your presentation than is generally true of large-group presentations. You may, for instance, fail to make a sale because the man who can make the decision was not invited to hear your presentation or is out of town or never received a copy of your written presentation.

In most organizations things get done by a subtle blending of authority, custom, and democratic cooperation. Even if you do have the official decision-maker at your presentation, you may draw a blank. He may refuse to commit himself because he wants to know what the persons who will carry out his orders think about the matter. You never thought of asking him to check the list of those who would be present.

In a presentation to a small group you must be even more sensitive to the attitudes of the audience than in a presentation to a larger group. This care must be heightened if your audience consists of one person or is dominated by one member. A preliminary scouting of the fellow who wanted to turn the cultural center into a trade-show exhibition hall might possibly have led to being ready for him with evidence that a cultural center, open the year round, would attract more visitors to Wheat City than a trade show now and then.

You should also try to learn in advance about personal quirks. One leading political figure prefers to study graphics silently—he snaps his fingers when he is ready for the next chart or slide. Knowledge of this disconcerting idiosyncrasy would lead to extra care with the graphics and a strong opening and closing.

Even when you are not dealing with any marked attitudes toward your subject or oddities of behavior, your presentation to a small group should be more personalized than it would be to an audience of a hundred. This more personal tone manifests itself in more constant awareness of individuals—frequent use of names, definite reference to their interests, more acknowledgment of their judgments, and so on. Suppose the trade-show enthusiast has no known interest in art, music, or the theater, but he is a collector of old clocks and a photographer of old buildings. You might discuss the possibility of his exhibiting his clocks and giving illustrated talks on the antiquities of Wheat City. This legitimate tie-in with your subject might do more to make him identify himself with your proposal than any argument about cultural needs of the city.

In a small group of several members you often must come up against divisions of opinion. Sometimes this division is only in relation to your subject. At others it reflects personal differences, sometimes of philosophy, sometimes of personality, sometimes of material interests, and sometimes of social groups. Not having found out about these cross-currents, you can founder and never know what sank you. Your position happens to please the Out-faction; therefore it must be opposed by the In-faction.

Realistically, you have little excuse to be caught in a situation of this sort unknowingly. When you know what the differences are, you take pains to indicate your personal objectivity by giving fair consideration to both sides of the question and by unruffled courtesy toward opposing views, even to the point of asking for them. If you cannot deal with them, you should not be making the presentation.

Sometimes on a public occasion—say that you are called as an expert witness in a trial or a hearing before a legislative body—

you will believe that your very integrity is being attacked. You have to remind yourself that the only way you can demonstrate your superiority to boorishness is through remaining calm and well-mannered. Persons who try to irritate you into confusion often make speeches along with their questions. You may hold on to your poise, slow down the pace of the attack, and score on the other side by quietly repeating the question with a rising inflection. This may lead the other side into confirming what may be a bald absurdity.

Once, for instance, a prosecuting attorney tried to upset an English professor who had testified for the defense on the interpretation of an old statute. After several leading questions, he asked sarcastically, "Would you call yourself an entomologist, professor?" The professor diffidently asked him to repeat the question. The attorney did with gusto. Then the professor repeated, "Would I call myself an entomologist?" He paused and said blandly, "No, sir, I would not. Why do you think I might be a student of insects?" The judge laughed, and the prosecutor abruptly ended his questioning.

Run Presentations to Small Groups in a Businesslike Way

You, not the audience, may be guilty of succumbing to informality and thus spoiling the effectiveness of a presentation to a small group. You would ordinarily not dream of taking two or three hours to make a presentation to an audience of 100. Presentations to small groups frequently run that long. Yet those to small groups habitually take place during working hours; those to large groups often on special occasions away from regular work.

Because you are politely received in pleasant surroundings, you may grossly misunderstand the situation. As you relax and use up valuable time on small talk, anecdotes, and longer than necessary explanations, your host may be looking for a reason to conclude the meeting, thinking up an excuse for leaving you to talk to an assistant or two, or crossing you off his list permanently. Because you have traveled 500 miles to make a presentation to an individual or a group, for instance, does not give you the right to spend the morning, if an hour is all you need.

Many small-group presentations require discussion as you go along. They are still presentations with purposes and patterns. Just because you are talking to one customer or three colleagues does not give you any excuse for a disorganized presentation. Always begin by making clear what you are trying to accomplish and hold to a controlling purpose and a one-two-three plan of development. The informality of an office or conference room, especially with persons you know well, allows discontinuity to creep into any presentation.

You have several ways to offset this danger:

Have your plan and your evidence so firm in your mind that you can keep the discussion on the track.

If the situation permits, use graphics in order to keep what is to be accomplished before the group.

Do not rehash points already covered. If you reach your objective—a sale or agreement on a proposition—before your presentation is finished, wind it up. Do not go through every step just because you planned it that way.

When your presentation is over, get out. Do not stand around repeating: "Well, we'd better meet again Thursday." End your meeting with a clean-cut understanding about what happened and what happens next. Then get out the door without lingering. Do not misconstrue your host's courteous remarks as an invitation to hold a farewell party in his doorway.

When you go into a small outside meeting with some of your associates, remember the suggestions made in Chapter 4 about presentations by groups. Be sure to have your signals straight. Who is the quarterback? What exactly do you expect to accomplish? Who talks about what? If notes should be made, who makes them? If a decision has to be made, what is it likely to be? Who makes it? What will the next step be?

Failure to abide by an agreed-on time schedule is probably the most common spoiler of presentations by more than one person. Recently the dean of a school of engineering invited a group of production men from the local industries to a luncheon on the campus to hear about a new curriculum. He feared that they probably would consider it unsound. Well in advance he and three department chairmen carefully planned their after-lunch presentation. The dean would take five minutes to sketch the main features of the new plan. Each of the chairmen would have ten minutes to cover his part of the curriculum. That would leave fifteen minutes for questions and summing up. The industry men could go back to work by 1:30 P.M., the usual time to end service club and similar noon meetings.

The luncheon started promptly at 12:05 P.M. and ended at 12:45 P.M. The dean took ten minutes instead of five—12:55 P.M. Then Professor A eased into his assignment with a couple of classroom jokes, restated what the dean had said, with additions— 1:10 P.M.; then, taking off, he delivered a 50-minute lecture— 2:00 P.M. As soon as he stopped, two guests excused themselves. The other professors abridged their talks drastically. The dean hurriedly answered one or two perfunctory questions and closed the meeting—2:10 P.M. Result: a disaster. The production men were annoyed at being kept longer than they expected; they did not understand the new curriculum well enough to consider it an improvement over the old one; and they had confirmed a feeling that professors are a feckless lot.

Listening Is Part of Small-Group Interaction

Listening has special importance during any presentation where the audience takes an active part. Selling and negotiation are characteristic occasions of this sort. Take this example. An advertising salesman for an FM radio station calls on the manager of an oscillograph plant. He wants the plant to sponsor a series of talks on science. After he has heard the carefully rehearsed presentation, the manager says, "I don't think we'd care to sponsor that sort of program." The salesman repeats his argument that the program would encourage the study of science in the schools and thus further the interests of the company. He does not make a sale.

The salesman's trouble is that he does not "read" the message the manager sends him. He does not really listen. He does not analyze what he hears: "I don't think we'd care to sponsor *that sort of program.*" He does not ask why not or what sort of program the company might sponsor. Had he done so, he would have learned that the manager feels his instrument company is so much identified with science that it should avoid even the appearance of being indifferent to the other subjects that the schools teach. The manager would sponsor a classical music program, but the salesman never gives him a chance.

An Ozark tale fits many presentations. An idle fellow named Lissanbee was noted as a great talker. One day he met a talking turtle down by a muddy stream. The turtle said, "Lissanbee, you talk too damn much." Lissanbee rushed back to town and brought his cronies out to hear the marvelous talking turtle. But the turtle did not say a word, so the other loafers threw Lissanbee into the muddy water and went back to town. As Lissanbee ruefully dragged himself out, the turtle said, "I told you, Lissanbee—you talk too damn much."

A presentation to a small group generally involves interaction. You may, for instance, make a presentation to fellow members of the governing board of a community fund. As president, you are submitting a proposal to hire a professional manager to head the fund campaign in the coming year. It is imperative that you handle your presentation with businesslike dispatch, just as though the other members are not friends of yours. Nevertheless, in this sort of situation you are probably as concerned as the rest of the group that the proposal be well aired and, if necessary, modified before it is adopted. Your presentation is only your share in the group activity. You are contributing, not persuading. You would like to have the board reach a unanimous decision.

In such a situation or in any other where interaction among all the members of the group—not just between you and them— goes on, listening is a significant part of that interaction. The surest way to prove you are not a pro is to make a presentation with vigor and then slump into inattention or show impatience as members of the group exchange ideas about what you have said. Listening is much more than polite silence while someone else is

talking. It is a creative way of interacting with that person's thinking, whether or not he is addressing you. If you are in the room,
you listen.

Listen a) to what is actually said; b) to the meaning behind
the words. Make a practice of doing these two things, all the
time, not just when someone is speaking to you. After a while you
will be amazed at how often in small-group discussion what is
said is misunderstood and how often a statement does not cover
the true meaning. The failure to understand the literal meaning
of plain statements is sometimes unbelievable. It is not evidence
of lack of intelligence so much as it is lack of attention. Failure
to grasp the true meaning behind what someone says may represent lack of sensitivity, lack of concentration, and lack of understanding of human nature, as well as failure to listen.

Suppose that during the discussion of your proposal to hire a
professional manager of the community fund a member of the
board says, "People are going to say we are using their money for
fat salaries." What does he mean? What answer is indicated?
Until you are sure of the meaning behind the words, you have
no answer. He may merely be indulging in the meaningless cyni-
cism that people use to relieve the tension or tedium of small
group meetings. He may mean a bald statement with the unsaid
addition: "—But it isn't true. We'll take care of that." Perhaps
he means something hidden. Possibly he feels that a professional
manager will downgrade his importance as a board member, and
so he is trying—unconsciously perhaps—to discredit the proposal
without openly attacking it.

As Chairman, You Can Help Make a
Presentation a Success

Chairmanship is a role you may play at a presentation. It has
two important aspects—getting the presentation started and guiding its progress. In other words you have responsibility for the
show.

Your job therefore starts far enough ahead to make sure that
the participants have all the information necessary for intelligent
planning. A good deal of preliminary exchanging of ideas should

precede any planning of specific presentations. You should share in the strategy analysis and not leave that to the speakers.

When possible, you should be present at rehearsals to help the speakers. Take a stop watch with you and time them exactly.

If several speakers are to be heard, estimate the time needed for their presentations, for discussion, and for coffee breaks. Be realistic in your figuring. Consult the speakers and insist that they stay within the time limit. Distribute the agenda ahead of time, if desirable.

Well before a formal presentation—long enough before to make a change, if necessary—check the room, audio-visual aids, and all details. Try out the public address system yourself. Do not meet in the midst of a lot of empty chairs.

Be ten minutes early to meetings where you are chairman. Start on time.

Do not prolong personal courtesies or irrelevancies at the outset. Get going.

If the agenda for the meeting has not been prepared ahead of time, it is sometimes worthwhile to review the presentations to be made before proceeding. Such a foreview will ensure that everyone knows the purpose of the meeting and how much has to be covered before it can adjourn. Taking part in a meeting which has not been oriented at the start is like trying to play chess without setting up the pieces in their proper places.

In opening a meeting, first gain the attention of the group. Do not mutter a weak, "Well, I guess we'd better get going" as though something unfortunate is about to happen. Try a) to put everyone at ease and b) to introduce the subject or problem in proper perspective. Be cheerful, businesslike, and brief. *Do not steal a speaker's thunder or his time.*

Carefully prepare your introduction of a speaker. Do not foul up his name, record, or topic. How would you like to be introduced as Robert Foster when your name is Foster Roberts? Stress the speaker's authority in the field. Do not be cute at a speaker's expense. On the other hand do not solemnly read his record as though you are reading his obituary. Do not insult him by a fatuous remark to the effect, "I don't know anything about Mr. Kay, but I'm sure we'll all be interested to hear what he has to say."

Pronounce the speaker's name clearly and more than once, whenever the audience may have difficulty catching it.

Time is your responsibility. You must be fair to the speaker, and you must be fair to the audience. Watch the clock. Be courteous but firm about keeping speakers to their allotted time. If you run the question period, restate the questions clearly; try to cover as many as possible. When time is up, thank the speakers warmly and recognize their specific contributions. Avoid soggy remarks, such as "I'm sure we all got something from your presentation." Close the meeting on time.

If you are chairman of a small-group presentation, you may have to exert more skill than at a large meeting. You have a good deal more to do about the climate and conduct of such a meeting. Say you are a salesman who has arranged to have two lab men discuss a technical problem at a customer's plant. It is up to you to see that the right people are there and have enough time set aside. You have to brief the lab men on who's who and do a careful situation analysis for them.

It is up to you to see that the presentation runs in the most effective way. In one instance, this may mean that you let the customers take the lead in raising questions. In another it may be necessary for you to play a straight man to the lab men—that is, ask questions you believe the customers ought to ask, suggest additional points the lab men might cover, and clarify possible misunderstandings.

As chairman of a presentation by several persons, it is your responsibility to keep track of how the scheduled sections proceed. Be sure that major matters get major attention. Do not let trifles and side issues force you to hurry main issues.

Do not let side conversations take place while someone is making a presentation or discussing one. Encourage only one person to speak at a time. Remind the group courteously how the time is passing and what presentations remain to be taken up.

If you are chairman of a panel of speakers, be sure that each has his share of the time. Be sure each is close to the microphone before he speaks. Invent questions, if necessary, so that all members of a panel take part in the question and answer periods.

At a small-group presentation, whether you are officially chairman or not, you can help make the occasion a success by accepting your responsibility for seeing that the discussion moves along according to plan.

In discussion never ignore what someone else is saying. Relate what he says to the general problem. If possible, show what is constructive about what he has said and build on it. Some of the time wasted in discussion comes from leaving points up in the air and having to backtrack to dispose of them. Sometimes they are insignificant; sometimes they are valuable. To the person who raises them, they are worthy of comment. To rush on with your ideas without acknowledging his, is boorish. You may create needless opposition. And you may reach poor or totally wrong decisions. It is discourteous not to give the other fellow a chance to talk—it can be disastrous if he is going to make the decision about your presentation.

Be slow to correct others or reject correction. You may be wrong. If you are wrong, say so—and express appreciation for the correction. Field all questions, especially complaints. Do something about complaints. Express concern. Clear up the trouble. Promise to do whatever is within your power to do. Write down the facts—pick up a phone and put through a call—do something.

Telephone Presentations Are As Important As Any Others

Some of your most challenging presentations take place over the telephone. You cannot always go to see someone on occasions requiring a presentation. You do not have the time. It is not economically feasible. Otherwise exactly the same conditions exist for a telephone presentation as for a personal one. (Telephone presentations normally involve an audience of one, though sometimes you might make more of an impression with a conference hook-up.) Many top executives—even heads of state—by choice, as well as by necessity, make and receive presentations on matters of great importance by telephone.

You may be inclined to discount the idea that telephone calls can rank as presentations. Think of typical presentation situations. The vice president of a lubricating company in Connecticut flies to Detroit to interest an automobile design staff in a new dry lubricant. A Georgia paper company sends an engineer to Chicago to convince the officers of a printing company that a $100,000 loss on a bad run of a magazine is not the fault of the paper. Now suppose, as is entirely possible, that these matters had to be handled by telephone. The vice president would have to present the same technical performance data and cost analysis to rouse the interest of an automobile designer. The engineer would have to marshal the same evidence of the innocence of the paper and perhaps the guilt of the ink, the humidity, or the presswork. And the outcome in both cases would be equally important.

Not all telephone calls are presentations by any means. Yet millions are. Telephone presentations are much more difficult to handle skilfully than others. Everything rests on the voice alone. You cannot count on the adventitious aid of how you look, a handshake, standing up, or audio-visual aids. You cannot read the expression of your audience. You hardly dare pause. You must condense your presentation ruthlessly. Your listener is free to make an excuse and hang up before you can finish your case. And you still must be exceptionally lucid and persuasive—all with your voice.

Just the same, telephone presentations have their own special challenge, even advantages. People do answer telephones in a compulsive sort of way, though they may be too busy to give you an appointment. They do listen to you when your voice comes out of a receiver held against an ear, though their minds may wander while they sit staring at you. On the other hand, you also may find that the presentation situation, abstracted to its essence, induces in you an unusual clarity and eloquence of expression.

Many of the techniques that make for excellence in other presentations apply to important telephone calls. Here are a few obvious but frequently violated rules:

In answering the phone or putting through a call, identify yourself first. Use your natural voice, not one from a sepulchre.

Speak clearly and courteously at all times. Do not convey the impression that your caller has interrupted something much more important than whatever he is talking about. Sound attentive and interested.

Before you place a call, be sure you know a) the name or title of the person to whom you wish to speak, and b) what you want to say to him.

A written checklist of points to be covered in the proper sequence is both a desirable guide and a helpful record of your call. Use a large pad, not scraps of paper. Date all such records and be sure to put down what was finally agreed. It is easy both to misunderstand and to forget what is said in telephone conversations.

Before you end an important call, review what has been agreed. A memorandum or letter confirming what was decided during your telephone conversation, with carbons to other persons involved, is often desirable. It should be dictated promptly before the meaning of your notes fades out.

On an incoming call, have the other person identify himself at once—name, company, title or department—and the general nature of his problem. Write this information down legibly on a clean pad. Use the other person's name occasionally as you talk. Your presentation loses its edge when the other person knows you do not know who he is.

Do not start solving a problem until you get it straight. Write down the facts as you listen. Read them back before you go further. Ask, "Is there anything else?" Above all, do not cut your caller short. Listen till he has finished, especially if he has a complaint. Be agreeable, never hostile or defensive.

If you are sure you know the answer, say definitely what you will do. Do not go back over the same ground. Many persons reveal their insecurity in dealing with problems by becoming repetitious on the telephone.

If you are not sure of the answer, say what you will do to find out and when you will report back. Keep your word. If you have to call back, be sure you have the correct phone number, including area code and office extension.

Do not prolong telephone calls unnecessarily. You may block an important call from getting through to you. Long distance calls may cost a company $100,000 a year, and be worth every dollar—but not if $40,000 has been spent unnecessarily. The standard three-minute call tends to run to five minutes.

Part IV

Written

Presentations

14

Forms of Written

Presentations

Your most effective oral presentations, we have said, should sound spontaneous. You cannot sound that way while you are obviously dependent on a written script. You, like the President of the United States, give greater evidence of knowing what you are talking about when you look constantly at your audience, and when you consult your knowledge of the subject, not your script.

Some Presentations Must Be Written

Yet, as we have conceded, a large percentage of presentations, probably most formal ones, are written first. If the material is unfamiliar or abstract, if it deals with sensitive matters, or if it calls for eloquence, written scripts are natural beginnings. They may be read word for word, glanced at for reassurance, or discarded before delivery time.

Some presentations must be written. Legal briefs, for example, often have to be submitted ahead of the presentation of a case in court. Apart from this type, however, you may have to prepare a presentation for someone else to give. Then you seldom have much choice besides writing a script as the basis for the other person to master the material. There are other times, important ones, when you will submit your presentation in writing, whether or not you make an oral one. You may do so by request, or you may do so because you want to. And you may do so before or after an oral presentation. Many offers to sell services are of this type.

What special considerations does a written presentation raise? In a sense they seem slight. You must gather and organize your material precisely as discussed in Part I, yet you must depend entirely on the eyes of your audience to comprehend your message. You can use illustrations, but you have to depend on an inflexible text to inform and persuade. Therefore your words and their arrangement count heavily. The physical form in which you submit a written presentation almost always counts. It is one of the areas where you can seek to add quality beyond the statement of your case.

Let us take an ordinary situation where a written presentation is in order. If you were the chairman of the Detroit Olympics Committee charged with making a presentation to the International Olympic Committee with a view to secure the Olympic Games for your city, you would certainly expect to leave with the IOC a written version of your oral presentation. Knowing the nationality of the members, you would translate your written statement into two or three foreign languages. You would include many illustrations—photographs of Detroit's existing attractions and an architect's drawings of facilities promised. You would distribute a large number of copies of your written presentation to the press and to government officials and Olympic committees all over the world who can influence the decision of the IOC. With an estimated $150 million addition to the economy of Detroit and many permanent benefits, such as new athletic buildings, hotels, highways, and civic improvements, the stakes are too high to depend on one formal oral presentation alone.

In situations such as the one facing this committee, the written form is the substance and often the literal form of the presentation. It is left to be studied, together with a contract; it is the legal offer. We must remember that the essence of a presentation, what gives sanction to the use of the word, is its serious concern to get a predetermined response from a specific audience. For that reason *memoranda, business letters, reports, technical and professional papers,* and certain other published *articles* can be considered written presentations. They also frequently use charts, graphs, drawings, and photographs as visual aids.

Memoranda, business letters, and reports are in many instances the equivalents of oral presentations to individuals and small groups. Technical and professional papers and certain other published pieces are aimed at larger audiences. The substitution of audience for reader, as has been observed, is a liberty commonly taken.

Memoranda Are Often Internal Presentations

The terms memorandum and report sometimes blur, because a report is sometimes submitted in memorandum form. In the ordinary sense, a memorandum is short, informal, and ephemeral. But it is so often the vehicle for making presentations that you should consider it here. Reports will be taken up later.

Your most common and vital presentation use of the memorandum is to submit recommendations within an organization. Numerous as meetings are, you cannot always catch one busy executive at your pleasure, let alone make an oral presentation to several. Instead of taking up an hour of a busy person's time presenting a complex problem and your solution to him orally, you can give him a written statement so compact and clearly organized that he can read in a few minutes what you may have spent days writing. He can read it at his leisure, re-read it, refer it to someone else, use material from it, and file it for future reference.

Instead of bringing together several members of an organization, you can reach them with a written presentation in memorandum form. You may do this because you are not able to bring them together. They may be far apart geographically, or no time for a meeting is open. Maybe you do not have the authority to call a meeting. Or you may prefer to keep these colleagues apart.

Knowing their personalities, you may believe you can get a better hearing for your case if each one reads it without being influenced by the reactions of others, especially the boss.

A memorandum is often the form used by an executive to communicate with the members of an organization. Typical situations are those affecting all or a large segment of the employees of a company. New programs for insurance, hospitalization, salary administration, profit sharing, sale of stock, safety, transfer of personnel, holidays, and shut-down of plants or offices have to be handled by written memoranda. On such occasions the supervisors should make an oral presentation, but they should have a memorandum from a top executive to read at the time. If this executive memorandum is not thought of as a presentation, but is a laconic bulletin, misunderstanding and trouble often result— even when the action to be taken is beneficial to the group.

In fact, executive announcements do tend to be misunderstood. They are often written by members of the personnel or legal departments who prefer the jargon of their trades to straightforward English. And they often depend too optimistically on accompanying oral presentations made by persons with incomplete understanding of the subject or with little commitment to it. Since, in addition, executive memoranda of this type are given or sent to all employees who are affected by them, they should be written with the same effort to make them understandable and persuasive as though they stood alone.

Memoranda May Be Advance or After-the-Fact Presentations

More routine situations are nevertheless important, too. Basically a written presentation is needed for internal purposes when the material covered is complex. The members of a management group, for instance, may have been discussing the progress of the negotiating of a new union contract for several weeks. When the industrial relations director presents the final terms, therefore, he has above everything else to be clear. He may use charts, slides, or overhead projection to highlight the key issues. But the group would expect a memorandum to supplement his clarification of the key issues of the contract. The memorandum would probably weigh the consequences of the changes and present the reasons for accepting them.

In an instance of this sort, where matters of weight are at stake and where thoughtful judgments have to be rendered, distribution of a covering memorandum in advance is often highly desirable. In such a situation failure to do so often signifies poor staff work. The time at such a meeting should not be taken up by an oral presentation to acquaint the group with the facts. The time should be given to discussion of alternatives and consequences and implementation.

Memoranda often follow problem-solving and decision-making meetings. They then are in fact written presentations of the sense of the meeting. Since many meetings within an organization are exceedingly informal and since the interest in the matters covered may vary widely, you often have a chance to make a valuable contribution by writing a memorandum of your interpretation of what took place. Without such an after-the-fact presentation you might later have difficulty getting some persons who were present to remember what went on. Perhaps they were not listening; perhaps they did not really understand; perhaps they prefer not to remember. At any rate your memorandum may pull together, clarify, and interpret in a way that mere minutes would not do.

Memorandum writing following problem-solving and decision-making meetings can approach creativeness when the matter of the meeting has to be transmitted to others not present. You have to draw on your imagination to estimate their knowledge of the subject, their prejudices, and their expectations. You have, in short, to realize that you are not merely recording what your group concluded. You have to imagine that you are making a face-to-face presentation and put the findings of your meeting into the form appropriate to your readers.

For example, you may be a member of a marketing group given the task of making a recommendation to a product manager about a new product. Your group takes an entire day to evaluate the technical reports and marketing studies that have piled up during the two years the product has been under scrutiny. The decision is no. Your memorandum to the product manager need not review all aspects of the problem investigated by the marketing group. Neither should it make a bald negative recommendation.

You would take into consideration that the product manager had high hopes of this new product and had given his superiors optimistic reports about it. Therefore, as you write your memorandum to him, you might summarize all the strong points about the product before indicating what last-minute evidence—a cheaper new competitive product—led to an adverse recommendation. The product manager may not like the recommendation, but he will not be embarrassed by your memorandum and have to write his own paraphrase of it to pass along.

As noted earlier, a memorandum distributed to your colleagues in advance of a negotiating session can be a position paper. This is an analysis of the issues being negotiated and a statement of the position of both sides on each issue. It also presents the steps your side will take to counter any moves that might be made by the other side.

Memoranda are usually read as part of the day's routine. The reader is not in a mood to have to dig the message out of a mess of verbiage. Because memoranda often cover several points in a summary way, they lend themselves to numbering, sub-heading, short sentences, short paragraphs, and other aids to quick reading.

Memoranda too often are longer than necessary, and they meander like a salt river through the marshes. Often tentative ideas are introduced early, and the decisive one is buried in the middle. The fact that you dictate or that you are in a hurry as you write is no excuse for inflicting your first thoughts on your readers. Organize your thoughts on cards before you dictate or write. If the first draft is too long or not clear, rewrite it. One good trick is to write a summary of a long memorandum and then let it become the memorandum. Triple-spacing first drafts makes revising easier.

Make clear at the outset of every memorandum what it is about. You can do this in two ways. Put the word "Subject" at the top left of the paper under "To" and "From," and after it state as precisely as possible what the point of the memorandum is. For instance, suppose that your organization has been considering for months a difficult problem about which many memoranda have already been written. Your memorandum may be more certain of attention if you label it "A New Solution to the Roberts Proposal" than if you repeat "Roberts Proposal."

Your second device for immediate clarification, especially when misunderstanding may be serious, is to list references to or mention previous correspondence, publications, or conversations, including dates. Often you need to summarize such material succinctly because your reader may not be acquainted with your references. Or your interpretation or memory may not tally with that of others.

Always put the essential point of your memorandum in the first sentence. In usual organizational circumstances, nothing is gained by building up to a recommendation or other conclusion. Your reader may never get there. Better to have the courage of your convictions and start out: "Because of the lack of a better alternative, I believe we should accept the Roberts proposal. If we do not, the consequences will be . . ."

Such forthrightness may not be at all appropriate in a presentation addressed to someone outside your own organization, but your own colleagues will be exasperated if you delay telling what you really have in mind. If they outrank you, they may do you the kindness of asking you to rewrite your thoughts without beating about the bush—or the unkindness of not even being that curious.

Letters Often Present Proposals

Much of what has just been said about memoranda applies to business letters. The significant difference is that letters go to outsiders. They are often presentations—sometimes the only ones you are permitted to make. What reactions they create can be a matter of considerable importance.

Every professional letter you write represents not only you, but also the organization to which you belong. We all tend to look on a letter from a department store, a professional firm, or a government agency as embodying the official voice of that organization, no matter how minor the clerk who drafts it. Indeed, business organizations encourage this interpretation by placing the name of the firm over the signature of the writer. As a matter of fact, a business letter from an employee is a legal commitment by the firm.

Chief among letters that are genuine presentations is the one that submits a proposal. Suppose, for example, that you read in a newspaper that the marble of the Parthenon on the Acropolis in Athens is deteriorating. You are the technical director of a firm that manufactures protective coatings for many specialized purposes. You believe that you might be able to stop further deterioration of the marble. You write a letter to the chairman of the commission mentioned in the news story. This letter is a presentation. Why?

To get results and to avoid misunderstanding, you would have to present the following: the reason for your interest, the reputableness of your firm, the technical capability of your staff, your experience in protective coatings, your success with the preservation of marble without discoloration, the names of public monuments on which your coatings have been successful, the information about the nature and extent of deterioration that you would require, the size of sample pieces of marble needed for analysis and tests, the conditions of your offer, and shipping instructions if your offer is accepted.

Completeness is a cardinal virtue of letter presentations. If you do not cover all of the points noted in your letter about the Parthenon, you may engage in long drawn out correspondence. Or you may be misunderstood to the extent of having your offer rejected because of doubts about your competence or your intentions. As a consequence, you fail in your effort to make a contribution to the preservation of one of the most important records of civilization. You also lose what would be worldwide publicity, if you were successful.

Executives write millions of presentation letters every day. As in the case of telephone calls, they are substitutes for face-to-face presentations. The most common, of course, is the sales letter. And it is the worst. The sales executive who would take considerable pains with a presentation he was going to make to a customer a thousand miles away may spend only twenty minutes dictating a letter to him. Direct-mail sales letters are precisely what we mean here by written presentations. Yet they are models of what not to do. They are long-winded, they are full of jargonish assertions with little concrete supporting evidence, and they show every evidence of being ground out in a tasteless, routine manner. A good sales letter has to be prepared in the same logical manner, with the same care, and with the same respect for the intelligence of the recipient as a good presentation in a customer's conference room.

The tone of a presentation in letter form often has crucial importance. Suppose you apply for a job by letter. Your letter is your proxy. You are presenting yourself by means of your letter. You must of course make clear why you are qualified for the job. And your letter must be impeccable in appearance and in English usage.

Beyond these absolutes is the more difficult matter of conveying a favorable impression of the kind of person you are. Most letters of application seem written by the same colorless person on the same poor grade of paper. For most purposes a letter of application flawlessly typed on heavy bond typewriter paper is acceptable. But suppose you are applying for the position of director of a museum. Then an engraved letterhead and a baronial (nearly square) envelope might be an appropriate part of your presentation.

More difficult is the feat of making what you say and how you say it speak favorably for you. Your letter of application for the job of a museum director, for example, should convey the idea that you are a cultivated person with sound professional training and experience. To achieve this impression, you would have to do more than state your case in a matter-of-fact way. On the other hand, efforts to attract attention in a letter by crude advertising-copy devices reflect inexperience and poor taste. In the next chapter is a discussion of how style can have character and reflect your personality.

In no presentation do you ever ignore the audience. In a letter of application, where you are presenting yourself, you must analyze your audience and apply what you learn. Yet few letters of job applicants ever show evidence of such effort. You improve your chances significantly if you take the two following steps: a) Address your letter to a specific person, preferably the person who has authority to hire you. b) Show that you are more than superficially acquainted with the activities of the particular organization to which you are applying. You would of course be as definite as possible about the job you want and your education and experience as proof of your competence to hold it. But in addition the two recommendations can make a big difference.

What is your reaction when you get a letter that is not addressed to you by name? Take the endless flow of direct-mail sales letters to "Householder" or "Purchasing Agent." You feel a certain amount of irritation, even a feeling that you have been affronted, somewhat as you do when some fellow wearing an official badge yells, "Hey, you!" at you for parking your car at the wrong angle.

More seriously, most applicants for jobs leave out of their presentation letters any proof that they know anything specific about the organization that allegedly they are willing to spend their lives working for. Often, in fact, they do know nothing beyond the name, and they copied that from a list. Yet with little trouble they could find out a good deal about any organization through inquiry and library research.

If they cannot bother to do that much about a matter so critical in their own careers, the recipient of the letter might ask, what is it that they can do? The recipient is certainly going to analyze that letter for clues to the person who wrote it. A presentation so impersonal that it shows no awareness of either the audience or the situation is just as bad in letter form as it is in a face-to-face confrontation.

The objective of a good letter presentation, therefore, is to create some of the atmosphere and the directness of interaction of an interview. You may say that this is impossible in a letter that must contain so much matter-of-fact material. The answer is—put the routine material in a one-page resumé and write a fresh two-paragraph letter of transmittal to every person to whom you are applying. The essential message may remain the same, but you should learn enough about each recipient to introduce a convincing specific reference or two. If you have not time to do that much for yourself, you probably are too busy to be looking for a job.

Reports Are Formal Presentations of Findings and Recommendations

Not all memoranda are presentations, but all reports are. Reports are formal in tone; they are the result of extensive research, investigation, or experience, often over substantial periods of time; and they usually run from several pages to book length. A short report transmitted in a memorandum form might as well be called a memorandum. The distinction is unimportant.

Report writing is a way of life for all professional men. An auditor does not finish his audit until he submits a written report. When a government official makes an investigation, he writes a report. Before an occasional new product emerges, industry executives see little but reports in return for the hundreds of thousands of dollars spent on research and development. In fact, one estimate puts the average cost of each laboratory report around $35,000. Reports are more than busy-work for laboratory workers. They are valuable records of ground covered. A report on negative results may save hundreds of hours and thousands of dollars of profitless repetition. It may disclose incidental results of value in another context, or it may reveal an error and so lead to successful further efforts.

Reports are often much more than corporate memories. They are the basis for executive decision-making. The accuracy, comprehensiveness, logical clarity, and persuasiveness of a report can be a tremendous contribution in the decision-making process. As often as not, an executive or group cannot safely make an important decision without studying one or more reports.

A report can provide three things that administrative persons are often too busy to get firsthand: Background information, a summary of crucial data, and an analysis of the key problems. In business, a report may sum up extended investigation of the economic feasibility of buying another company, for instance, and thus be the critical evidence on which a decision involving millions of dollars is based.

Or a report may be used to buttress an oral presentation such as the kind made by management consultants to business firms at the end of an engagement. It may cost the client $50,000 and lead to permanent changes in the organization and the way of doing business for a large corporation. In government, a staff report may put forward the essential grounds for far-reaching actions.

When an executive feels that he can safely base his decisions on the reports submitted to him, he has an exhilarating sense of confidence in his staff. The writing of excellent reports has been the stepping-stone to posts of high command for many a previously obscure person, including Dwight D. Eisenhower. On the other hand, the number of careers blighted by poor reports has mercifully gone unrecorded.

Since most reports are written for specific readers, including your boss, find out exactly what their preferences are and meet them. If a set format exists, as it often does, follow it. If you have no established format to follow, ask yourself what your particular readers probably want to know about your subject. Stress that and leave out or play down what they are not likely to want to know.

If no approved form exists, make up a logical one. To whom is the report addressed? Who is making it? What is the precise nature of the subject? Why was the reported activity begun? What procedures were followed in gathering data? What are the results? What do they mean? What is their importance? What is the relation of the matter reported on to other matters of concern to the recipient of the report? Do you have any recommendations? If so, what are they? What evidence and what reasoning support your recommendations? What plans for further investigation do you have? What authorities have you consulted?

It is standard practice to start a report with a one-paragraph *abstract* of aim, activity covered, findings, inferences, and if appropriate, recommendations. Include essential facts. A good abstract is your best assurance a) that you have mastered your subject, b) that the message of your report will register, and c) that it will be understood. Even then, when a report is long—

say over ten pages—and filled with technical data, it is often wise to follow your abstract with a *summary* of a few paragraphs.

You increase readability by breaking up pages of copy with headings and subheads. One customary system is to put main headings in capitals in the center of the page, subheads with initial capitals flush at the left margin, and secondary subheads indented and underlined. Your material may require some other system. Your system should be consistent, and it should be visually helpful.

A report is usually a working paper. It is not the occasion for total recall or for elaborate refinements. Your thought should be clear and logical, and your style plain, precise, and succinct. The final decision about a recommendation in a report may be made by a non-technical man. Explain technical terms, if your readers are not familiar with them.

If graphs, tables, photographs, or other illustrative material can make a primary contribution to your message, they should be as close to the related passage in the text as possible. If the contribution is secondary, they should not clutter the main part of the report, but should be exhibits or appendices at the end of the body of the report. In either case the text should include a clear reference to the illustration, e.g., see pg. 1; see exhibit A. For drawings use only India ink or other dark ink that reproduces well. Reports are often reproduced after you have distributed them.

A long report should have a title page and a table of contents.

Date your report. Undated reports can be dangerous as well as worthless. They may be used after they have been superseded. They may be used as reference years after they are written.

Many times an unwieldy report that cannot be shortened can be turned into an effective presentation by dividing it. You can put the essential message in the body and much of the supporting evidence and amplification of ideas in an appendix. In technical reports, tables and experiments may often be relegated to appendices.

Reports are often bound in various ways for permanent reference. Therefore you should leave a margin of one inch and a half on the left. When you include graphs or other illustrations, do not write in this margin. Put captions and keys above or below the illustration. Put as little writing as possible within the graphic design.

A binder will suggest the respect you feel for your work. Reports may be stapled in the blue backing paper of the sort lawyers use, but more elaborate binders may be desirable. A report that has cost hundreds or thousands of dollars is worth a $1 binder. Many organizations have specially designed binders.

Observe strictly all security regulations. In industrial and government organizations, procedures for safeguarding confidential reports are generally carefully prescribed.

Reports are often the result of committee or other group thinking. It is generally advisable, however, to have one person write the first draft of the report, receive the criticisms of the other members, and then produce a final draft. Communal authorship is not an efficient way to write reports.

In certain government agencies and management consulting firms it is standard practice to submit a trial draft of a report to the recipient. The trial really is as near final as the writer and his colleagues can make it. It is simply not dressed up in a good binding or processed in multiple copies. The recipient is invited to look it over and to make suggestions. This procedure enables the recipient, in effect, to reject the report temporarily and the writer to make changes with face-saving grace. Or it gives a guarantee of acceptance before official submission. Your situation analysis will tell you whether or not such a tactic can be useful to you on a specific occasion.

Technical and Professional Papers Are Presentations to Peers

Technical and professional papers are prepared for delivery at meetings of technical and professional societies, trade groups, government and educational bodies, and similar specialized gatherings. They are generally regarded as presentations. They often include illustrations and call on audio-visual aids when delivered, but they also commonly advance a thesis of some sort that the author seriously wishes his audience to accept. For instance, in a professional society meeting a doctor or scientist may sum up his research for a year or more. He hopes that his peers will grant the validity of his conclusions. At a trade-group meeting an engineer may review the performance capabilities of a new product. He hopes that the audience will sample his product and then adopt it.

But technical and professional papers are broader means of communication. Because the audience understands the subject presented, papers are the basis for judgments about the competence of the persons who write them and about the stature of the organizations represented. At all national professional society meetings each neophyte and veteran faces a roomful of competent and not always charitable critics. They are all from Missouri.

The man who does well will get compliments from the persons best qualified to know how sound, original, and important his research has been. These are the three criteria by which technical or scholarly presentations are judged—soundness of the research, its degree of originality, and its relative importance. In addition, inevitably, members of professional society audiences are keen judges of the organization and handling of presentations. One paper, therefore, that gets a high rating on all counts may do much to make the writer's reputation, lead to his acceptance by fellow-workers in a field, or bring offers of new positions.

Technical and professional papers should be written with care because, even though they may not be read in their entirety at a meeting, but only summarized orally, they are often published in the official journal of a society or in another appropriate publication. A society usually stipulates that its journal has first option on all papers. It is, however, often possible for you to receive permission in advance to dispose of your paper elsewhere where it will do you or your organization more benefit.

The publication procedure in force in your own organization usually makes certain that you will receive advice about the disposition of your papers. It is particularly important that your public relations or advertising department make suggestions. It is often much more valuable to an organization to place a paper in one publication rather than in another—it may be read by customers, it may have a circulation greater than any other in the field, and so on. Reprints may have valuable uses for years.

Instructions for preparing papers for technical and professional society publications vary with societies. They are usually extremely exacting about every detail, such as paper, illustrations, numerals, abbreviations, symbols, and footnotes. You should secure a copy of the appropriate style sheet before writing a paper.

Most professional societies require the submission of an abstract long before a meeting. It is sometimes used as a basis for deciding whether or not to invite you to present a paper. Abstracts are often printed in programs distributed before meetings occur. A hasty abstract, written before you have come to grips with your paper, may cut down your audience. It may also embarrass you by its inadequacy or by the limitations it imposes on you. Typical instructions for writing an abstract usually include the following:

Keep the length of the abstract within 300–400 words so that it will fit on a single page.

Submit an original and three carbon copies.

If more than one author is involved, underline the name of the author presenting the paper.

Submit final copy with no erasures or other corrections. Abstracts are often reproduced directly from copy. Corrections smudge in certain reproducing processes.

Enclose separate summary information about the author(s)— mailing address, age, education, degrees, business or professional connection and address, position, title, work experience, publications, and professional societies.

Non-Technical Articles May Be Presentations to the General Public

Many technical and professional articles are written directly for publication without being delivered orally. They do not differ significantly from those read or paraphrased at meetings. Non-technical articles and various other publications, however, are usually written for the general public, or a large segment of it such as women, not for specialists in plastic surgery, Slavic scholarship, or similar disciplines.

An important in-between article may be called the semi-technical. It is the kind that appears in some trade journals and in publications—*Scientific American* is an example—that are written for the serious, well-educated reader, but not the specialist. Many, but not all, trade journals publish articles only for the technical specialist. Most business executives, for instance, try to keep up with a wide spectrum of activities relevant to their affairs by means of a half dozen magazines and two or three newspapers that publish serious articles about financial, political, marketing, and technological developments.

Non-technical and semi-technical articles offer an admirable means of widening the audience for executive presentations of all kinds. Most trade journal articles come out of technical work, such as that in product development laboratories. They are often about products, materials, and developments that will arouse interest in customers. But a good article by any executive contributes to the prestige of the organization for which he works, and it contributes to the professional standing of the author.

A paper is judged on its academic or professional merits. A non-technical article is judged first on its appeal to the readers of one magazine, as decided by the editors. It is not necessarily based on original research by the writer, but it should have a sense of newness to the readers. Two qualities of an article therefore get rigorous consideration—freshness of material and interestingness of writing.

Suppose you are thinking of writing an article. What steps do you take? You do not sit down and write it. You proceed somewhat as follows:

a) Study your material. Is it fresh? Do you know the subject thoroughly? Jot down your main ideas.

b) Go to the library. What magazines or newspapers publish articles of the sort you have in mind? In spite of the multitude of magazines published, most of them are highly specialized. An article that fits one magazine for persons interested in cosmetics may or may not be suitable for another also concerned with cosmetics.

Are articles in the appropriate magazines written by contributors? Many publications are entirely staff written. It is your business to know the publications that might publish your article.

c) Now you are ready to discuss your proposed article with someone who knows the subject and someone who knows the publishing situation. In industry this means with your supervisor and appropriate persons in marketing, advertising, public relations, or other relevant departments.

d) If the outlook is promising, you may submit your suggestion to editors and get an indication of interest before you invest more time in the project. If the material seems best placed in a staff-written magazine, you may still write it up in article form, or you may send your material in report or outline form. Sometimes what you think of as an article may best benefit your organization as a release to a wide variety of media, including newspapers and trade journals. Or both an article and a release may come from your idea.

Apart from content, *reader appeal, structure,* and *style* are the three main aspects of writing a magazine article.

Reader appeal is based on audience analysis. Your first step is to identify your readers in order to determine how to adjust your message to their comprehension and their interests. Who are your readers? What do they know about your subject? What do they want to know? What do you know that they want to know?

Analysis of articles in the few magazines where your article might be published is a *must* in helping you to fit your message to your reader. What is the average length? What is the level of technical sophistication? Are statistics, graphs, and illustrations used? Is the style academic or popular? Though some editors will rewrite good material, do not expect a magazine to change its policies to accommodate you.

Your analysis will determine a) what you include, b) what you leave out, c) what you emphasize by position in the article, by amount of space, and by extent of the claims you make, and d) what graphics you will need to illustrate your copy.

The relative brevity of most articles and the necessity to achieve comprehension and acceptance of your message make transparent clarity imperative. Therefore the structure must be simple.

Reduce your message to a single sentence. This is your controlling purpose. Remember: If you cannot sum up what you have to say in one sentence, you are not ready to write—or to ask an editor to consider having you write—an article. And remember, too: A controlling purpose is your topic, plus a statement that is both as inclusive and as precise as you can make it. "Industry faces growth problems in the next decade because of a shortage of skilled workers to operate new machines" might give the gist of an article in one sentence. Such a sentence planted in an early paragraph gives the reader his bearings through the rest of the article.

As discussed in Chapter 3, the elaboration of your message inevitably follows a simple one-two-three progression. Analysis of any subject reduces to (a) units and (b) aspects—that is, (a) things and (b) ideas about them. For instance, most technical articles reduce to (a) products or materials (units) and (b) their properties and applications (aspects). A little thought will tell you whether it is more effective to organize your article around (a) or (b).

The most logical and appealing organization of an article is most easily found by placing notes on cards and playing solitaire with them. This procedure is ten times easier than trying to add to or change the order of ideas written down on sheets of paper as they come to you. Making notes on cards allows you to think your way through your article painlessly—to add, subtract, and combine items and to decide on the sequence of items and whole blocks of materials. You generally think of more ideas than you should include—the history of your subject, for example, may be dispensable. It is a lot easier to throw away cards than to kill paragraphs of imperishable prose. This is the time to make sure you have the concrete evidence to support your generalizations, usually facts, statistics, comparisons, and examples.

When you have shuffled and labeled your cards properly, you have the makings of an outline and an abstract of your article. You will save time by writing both before you write the article. If at this point you are not able to write an outline and an ab-

stract, you are not ready to write your article. Re-think your
material step by step with your cards to guide you.

After you have written the first draft of your article, write
your lead. This delay will save you from an over-elaborate "introduction." The lead in a semi-technical article tells the reader
why he should read it. You tell him something such as how
certain processes or products will benefit him by solving his problems. A concrete example of their successful use to solve a real
or disguised customer problem is a standard lead. Other standard
leads are a) a tie-in with an item of timely interest, and b) a
striking claim of the significance of your subject.

In a popular article the lead more often aims at rousing interest. Dramatizing the material by starting with a typical example or building the entire article around one person or group
is universal practice. You will find this familiar lead acceptable
even in articles that present serious material to a specialized
reader. An article about the economic system of Yugoslavia might
well start with how one family in Zagreb exists.

Many persons who are busy constantly making oral presentations as part of their job or of their civic responsibilities never
give serious thought to writing articles. Yet one article can get
a message to as many thousands as a year of oral presentations
can. Perhaps you are a salesman. You wonder whether or not you
will be one all your life—all salesmen wonder about that. One
article in a magazine might create national interest in your company's products and interest in you at headquarters. It would be
a demonstration of your extra ability, and yet it would be merely
another form of presenting the material you present every day.

Perhaps you find yourself publicity chairman of a citywide
campaign to raise money for medical services to handicapped
children. In order to prepare the public for door-to-door solicita-
tion, you have to present your case. Beyond the normal channels
of publicity open to you, you could strengthen your cause immensely by means of a feature article in the Sunday magazine
supplement of the newspaper. It is the only newspaper printed in
your city, and everybody reads it. Why not? You could perhaps
persuade an editor to assign a staff writer to do the article. But

how much more satisfactory to be able to do the job yourself—and you may have to.

Merely sitting down and writing an exhortation to support the campaign is not enough. That is the privilege of the editorial writer only. The public must be made to understand the needs of the children, to feel compassion for them, and to want to help them. Your basic analysis suggests that you have three kinds of material to cover: a) the facts about handicapped children in your community, b) the need of medical services for their care, and c) human interest cases to arouse an emotional response. And you know that an anecdotal lead is appropriate. Some of the same visual material—figures and photographs, especially—that you would use in oral presentation would be incorporated in your feature article.

If you can get the time on radio and television, of course you do use speech—either that of an announcer or of a campaign worker. Then you can arouse a good deal of sympathy through the feeling in a voice. A television presentation would probably be reinforced by visual aids, just as any other oral presentation would be.

Releases and Brochures Extend the Reach of Executive Presentations

On many occasions releases sent to selected newspapers and magazines are true written presentations. Say that a long-established maker of garden tools in New Hampshire wishes to announce that it is diversifying its business by buying a seed company. The president calls a press conference. He gets up and presents the reasons for the action, the way the business will now be conducted, and the benefits to gardeners.

But this oral presentation suffers from two limitations. First, the president cannot expect to have present more than a handful of local news media representatives and maybe not one representative of trade and business publications. Second, he cannot expect reporters writing, according to their custom, on folded sheets of paper to get all the ideas and factual details as he would like to see them printed. By turning the notes for his oral presentation into a condensed written statement, he has a release to hand to those who attend the press conference and to send to those out-of-town publications that might consider the facts newsworthy.

A release must have some news content to justify an editor's printing it. The organization of a news story is more or less mechanical. You encapsulate the essential news in the opening —the traditional *who? when? where? what? why?* Then you cover the key elements succinctly. Finally you add the less significant details of the story and give background information.

This technique allows an editor to cut or condense your story without loss of the main features. If you put yourself in the place of the editor and keep your release to the length that its intrinsic news value justifies, you are likely to have it printed unchanged.

Presentations often are printed as brochures. (The root of the word in French means to stitch; a few printed pages stitched or stapled together are a brochure.) A bank may add insurance and annuity programs to its services. No oral presentation or other written presentation can meet this situation as well as a brochure. The audience are the thousands of bank depositors and persons whose names are on selected mailing lists. Each one can be mailed a copy, with a good chance that the message will be read. On other occasions a presentation in a brochure can be handed out at the end of an oral presentation. It then acts as a means of impressing on the audience the importance of the message and as a durable reminder of what was covered. It can also be passed on and so influence others.

Brochures are often extremely well written and handsomely printed. The reason is that the persons issuing a brochure are usually keenly conscious of what they are trying to accomplish. Most often they are trying to raise money, sell a service, interest the public in investing money, or create a favorable impression of an organization. They do not consider themselves competent to prepare a brochure. They therefore entrust the writing and design to professionals. Yet how rarely do the same people ask for professional help in their oral presentations or letters and memoranda?

You can see here a two-way proposition: If you need professional help in preparing a brochure, you need it for other presentations, which often have more crucial significance. On the other hand, if you are competent to handle other presentations, you can either prepare or direct the preparation of a brochure.

You face much the same questions you face in any presentation situation. Once more: Who will the readers be? What is your controlling purpose? What response do you wish to get? What is the 1-2-3 of your main ideas? What facts support your main points? How can you make your story interesting? Will illustrations help?—photographs, drawings, graphs, tables? How long should the brochure be? What should the format be—the size, shape, paper, typography? The designers of a brochure can do almost as much for the impact of your presentation as you can do through the message itself.

15

The ABC of Style

and Usage

Many executives go through high school, college, and various kinds of graduate schools innocent of trustworthy knowledge of English or how to write it. They literally play it by ear. For the last time we repeat our homespun definition of a pro—a person who knows what he is doing.

To make presentations of professional standard, you must know how to handle the English language. Therefore, in this last chapter let us review the ABC of style and usage.

You Can Develop a Professional Writing Style

A written presentation differs from other effective writing in greater effort to arouse a specific response in the reader. Otherwise it should meet the standards of good English style. No such thing as "business English" exists. Apart from its specialized vocabulary, the English of business and professional writing is either acceptable for almost any condition, or it is jargon—permissible as shop shorthand, but jargon nonetheless.

It is no exaggeration to say that American business and profes-

sional men and women have no writing style at all. Their prose
does not have marked lucidity, force, command of the felicitous
phrase, apt imagery, or graceful rhythm. The reason is that they
are strangers to the works of masters who have made the English
language a great instrument of human communication, as the
Germans have made music. Unconscious imitation is the foundation of all style. If you would make your own writing richer and
more skilful, read good literature—biographies, novels, essays,
plays, poetry—not just newspapers, magazines, and technical
books.

Ultimately a professional writing style is a studied matching
of subject matter, purpose, and the technical elements of style.
Suppose you have to make a written presentation of a proposal
to establish a new medical research institute in your city. First
you must know more about the proposed research and the functioning of an institute than your readers do. You also have to
have conviction about the purpose of such an enterprise. Only
then are you able to choose the stylistic effects necessary to
achieve the eloquence that may arouse equal enthusiasm in your
readers.

Probably the reason that so many written presentations are not
as effective as they should be is that most of us have the habit
of sitting down to write or to dictate without an organized plan
to guide us. The notion that what results from such a first draft
can be readily revised is a serious mistake. An unplanned first
draft has many illogical sequences, omissions, accidental empha-
ses, and mal-proportions. The only rewriting that makes sense is
to start all over with a clear plan and do the job right. It will help
to review Part I of this book before beginning any written presentations.

The act of communication is more complicated than merely
saying things. A listener or reader rarely completely grasps a
message that is made up of abstractions or general assertions. If
you really want your reader to grasp and remember what you
are writing, you will have to be concrete. A statement such as,
"In the age of chivalry, when knighthood was in flower, women
were little more than chattels," is understandable but not memorable. The idea lights up like a match in night shadows when

Elaine Kendall says, "The age of chivalry by definition refers to a time when men were kind to their horses."

Circumstances will sometimes force you to prepare a written presentation to read aloud—because of the precise timing of radio or television, for example. Or you may have to write a presentation someone else is going to read aloud. Then you write in a style that is easy to read aloud and that sounds as un-read as possible. Instead of saying, "Clare's pervasive sentimentality, to which Robinson alludes, is one intrinsic aspect of his romanticism," you might say: "Robinson refers to Clare's sentimentality. Clare's work is shot through with sentimentality. It is part of his romanticism." You write short units, repeat key words, substitute everyday words for formal words, and lighten the tone by idiomatic expressions like *shot through*.

A presentation to be read aloud is often written for an occasion where eloquence is in order. You can add eloquence to your style by two chief devices. First, you can find colorful words or phrases to heighten the effect at critical spots. Second, you can pay attention to the rhythm. For instance, take a random sentence by Henry Thoreau: "To a philosopher all news, as it is called, is gossip, and they who edit and read it are old women over their tea." Had Thoreau's style not been molded in an oratorical tradition, he might have written, "A philosopher considers news a form of gossip, and editors and readers little more than old women indulging in gossip." That is the essential idea in a straightforward statement. But it lacks color, and it lacks rhythm. Try reading the two versions aloud. See how Thoreau's rolls along in easy breath groups until it ends with the scornful whiplash "old women over their tea." Reading aloud is the touchstone of style.

First You Must Master a Sound Utility Style

But first, at a more modest level, you must master a sound utility style. You can do so by conscious attention to a few key matters in everything you write. Professional writers do.

Sentence length. Keep your sentences down to an average below 24 words, roughly two lines. You do this (a) by using the *fewest* possible words to express your ideas, and (b) by starting a *new sentence* when one is getting out of hand. The essence of professional writing lies in (a). Your style is right when no one can cut another word from it. "The results which were obtained . . ." is three words too long. Merely cutting meaningless qualifying words like *very, quite,* and *rather* will tighten up your style. But sentences and parts of sentences can be compactly written and still not say enough to be worth keeping. And long sentences can be so constructed that they are clear and easy to read aloud.

When you have a complete typed first draft of a written presentation, try this: Go through from beginning to end with just one objective—to shorten as many sentences as you possibly can. Do nothing else. Make just two changes: Cut out words. Divide each long sentence into two sentences. This can become a diverting game with illuminating results. Even fairly presentable sentences take on a lean and muscular look when they are subjected to this treatment.

Sentence order. Keep your sentences moving in a straight line. *Start with the subject, say something about it, and stop.* Put main ideas in main clauses: "Berzelius, a Swede, first freed elemental silicon from the silicon-oxygen bond." Not, "Berzelius, who first freed . . . , was a Swede." Avoid wind-ups such as "It is to be observed that."

A good utility style has a minimum of digressions. The more straightforward your style, the less you will need interior punctuation. Subordinate clauses, particularly *which* clauses, participial constructions, and parenthetic explanations tie kinks in sentences. Starting a new sentence unkinks many knotty constructions. Sometimes opening a new sentence with *but* or *and* avoids more complicated constructions.

Word choice. In professional presentations you may have to use a good deal of technical language. Therefore try to make the *filler words* in your sentences as light as possible.

Use plain English—*said* not *expounded, has* not *possesses, parts* not *components, cut down* not *minimize, best* not *optimum.* But be precise and accurate. "This investment should earn 7% interest" is exact; "a comfortable income" is not.

Use *that* to introduce restrictive relative clauses some of the time for variety. Do not use *which* all of the time. "This is the procedure that we followed."

Use active verbs when you can, not hind-end-to passive constructions. "The results justify further research." Not "Further research seems to be justified by the results."

Avoid overdoing impersonal *it* constructions. "Further research seems justified." Not "It would seem that further research is justified."

There is and *there are* often lead into word-wasting constructions: "There is reason to believe that the new equipment will probably be ready by August." The first six words are superfluous.

The roundhouse construction *as far as . . . is concerned* is both clumsy and pretentious. "Our ablative material meets NASA specifications" is much better than "As far as NASA specifications are concerned, our ablative material is acceptable."

Thought flow. You are traffic manager for your written presentation. At the outset you make clear to your reader what your purpose is and what main points you will cover. Then you use two kinds of *signals* to help him follow your thought flow: You repeat *key words* to keep clear what you are talking about at a given point.

You insert *pointer words* to show what direction your thought is taking. Take the sentence "Another application of resins in electronics is in radar equipment." The single pointer word *another* signals the reader that he has finished one thought and is about to start another. The rest of the sentence reminds him what he has been reading about and points to what he is now going to hear.

Your Writing Has to Pass the Glance Test

A piece of writing should be clear enough to pass what we might call the glance test. A businessman glances through his correspondence, a professional man glances at the articles in his technical journals, a housewife glances through a brochure from her alma mater.

Almost no one ever seems to do any steady reading at once. We all go through this scouting maneuver. We take a quick look at a written presentation to see, first, whether the subject is sufficiently related to our interests to be worth further attention. If it seems to be, our eyes skim over the page to pick up further clues as to whether or not it will be worthwhile to read the article carefully later on.

To deal with this reality of communication, you have to make sure that the clues can be picked up at a glance. What are they? First, the title must come as close as you can get to summing up the controlling purpose in three to five words. Here are a few good ones from the Harvard Business Review: "Where to Find Marketing Facts," "Is Management a Profession?", "Squeezing the Waste Out of Advertising," "Executive Compensation Here and Abroad."

Any subordinate captions should be meaningful to the glancer. Tables, charts, graphs, and other illustrations should yield a message to a wandering eye.

Your opening and your conclusion together should tell an experienced reader what aspects of your subject you cover and fairly well what you say about them.

Perhaps the most important part of the glance test is your style itself. If you write impenetrable prose full of long words and qualifying clauses, all beginning with *which,* your potential readers will miss the message and pass on. Keep your sentences reasonably short and unkinked, salt them with the words of ordinary speech, and refer often to the concrete aspects of your subject. Then the roving eye can seize enough of your message to make a just decision about the relevance and merits of your article.

Professional writing is about 50% preparation, 25% writing, and 25% rewriting. Clarity and economy and persuasiveness come only with much *editing* and *fresh drafts*. Reading aloud often helps you spot weakness in structure, style, or reader appeal. Having several competent critics read your manuscript is the best way of ensuring that it fulfills its purpose. Choose your critics for knowledge of your material, for professional writing ability, and for ability to imagine what your potential readers will think. Ask your critics to write their suggestions on a separate sheet of paper, not on your manuscript. As in every other field, you can be confident that your experience will bring you better performance.

Triple-space all first drafts, whether typed or handwritten. Then you can make corrections legibly. Before turning over a draft to a typist, proofread it. As you arrive at the final version of each sentence, black out every word that is not to be copied. Do not use parentheses. Use a marking crayon, an editor's pencil, or a felt pen. Draw heavy lines from a correction to where it is to be inserted. When extensive copy is to be inserted, cut up the MS. and paste the new copy in its proper sequence. You will get your copy typed faster and with fewer errors by following the suggestions in this paragraph. One or two errors on a page can mean complete re-typing and another proofreading.

Learn the proofreaders' marks in your dictionary. Distinguish between the directions to the printer that go on copy and the marginal indicators of corrections on proof. Do not use the latter —marks like ℒ and *tr*, that is—on copy; make the changes.

Acceptable English Usage Depends on Specifics

Acceptable English usage in written presentations is more critical than in oral presentations. Readers are much more sensitive to how words are used and to violations of the conventions of usage than listeners are. Put it another way: in a written presentation you have to concern yourself with a great many niceties of usage that probably do not bother you at all when you are making an oral presentation.

A scholarly survey reports that most persons who habitually say, "He ate *like* he had not seen food for days," switch to *as though* in formal writing. Is it wrong to use *like* as a conjunction? No. Historically it has been so used. Yet some handbooks condemn such use. Educated persons north of Baltimore avoid it in speech and in writing. Custom seems to limit its use to conversation among those educated persons who use the construction at all.

What conclusion can you draw from this simple example? Beyond the "I ain't seen him nowhere" level of illiteracy, slang, obscenity, and substandard gross errors, it is hard to make firm distinctions between correct and incorrect English. In fact, the notion that you can look up general rules and original historical forms to find out whether or not a construction is right or wrong reveals a misconception about the English language.

English usage is a body of specific practices. They change slowly but steadily through the generations. Their acceptability varies among different social groups and in different circumstances. These circumstances fall roughly into four levels of usage —formal (as in a presidential message), standard (as in most published non-fiction writing), informal (as in the conversation and friendly letters of educated persons and often for effect in other forms of writing), and substandard (as in the conversation of uneducated persons).

Thousands of expressions are acceptable at the informal level— folk idioms, such as "He was fit as a fiddle," for instance. A certain colloquialism may add just the right note to an oral presentation and sometimes to a written one. Or it may be completely inappropriate in both. The problem is the one of tone, discussed in the preceding chapter. A judgment has to be made about a specific usage in specific circumstances.

The best answer for you is to study the actual practice of editors, serious writers, scholars, and other discriminating users of the English language. A consensus of their ordinary practice is what most handbooks try to report. But what you find in one handbook or dictionary is not inevitably "right." Laymen often misunderstand reference books because they skip the introductory discussion. You also have to realize that, as in politics, authorities range from conservative to liberal. On top of that, they are not any more consistent than politicians. To decide whether or not you will make distinctions such as those between *shall* and *will*, *disinterested* and *uninterested*, *providing* and *provided*, you will have to do more than look up one reference.

But all the while the man in the street goes on using the English language as he sees fit, and slowly his practice begins to take effect. As the years go by, certain substandard expressions slowly become accepted in informal use and some even at the standard level. What people hear, they tend to use.

For instance, at the present time the average American has come to regard "there is" as a general signal, a sort of throat-clearing, not as an indication of a singular noun or pronoun to follow. It is therefore predictable that within the next twenty years a crudity such as "There is several applications for this material" will be acceptable in the conversation of educated persons and may be tolerated in serious writing.

Meanwhile, in addition to studying consciously specific practices in carefully edited newspapers, magazines, and books, you should also have at hand and consult regularly two or three standard handbooks and dictionaries. Many of the subtleties discussed will concern you only occasionally. Here are some of the most common problems of usage that you will meet in your written presentations:

a) Vocabulary

"He *effected* stringent economies that *affected* plant operations." As a verb *effect* means to bring about; *affect* means to change, pretend, or be fond of. The noun is *effect* except in a special use in psychology.

Do not use *infer* for *imply*. "When he *implied* that Jason was untrustworthy, I *inferred* that Jason had beaten him at checkers."

Contact as a verb, as in "Contact the dealer," has wide acceptance in business communication and informal conversation but not otherwise. Why not use *meet, get in touch with, call,* or *write?*

Sort of or *kind of* in the adverbial sense—"I sort of like London"—exists in the informal speech of some educated persons but not in their formal writing. It is a weak meaningless expression. "London is the sort of [not sort of a] city I like" is standard usage.

"We ordered a special *type of material.*" Not *type material.*

Conservative authorities deplore *due to* used in any way besides the adjectival: Acceptable: "Increased profits are not always due to increased sales." Try using *because of* in adverbial constructions: "The Tigers lost because of their lack of hits."

Temperature is always *high, low,* or *moderate.* Not hot, cold, or warm.

Speed and *velocity* are always *high* or *low.* Not fast or slow.

"The foundation is *providing* $1 million, *provided* the college raises $3 million." *Provided* is the form to use for *on condition that.*

" 'The *principal* reason for this punishment is the *principle* of the thing,' the school *principal* said." *Principal* means chief; *principle* means a truth or law.

b) NUMBER

This kind (*sort*) is singular; *these kinds* (*sorts*) is plural. Not *these kind*.

"The teacher, the students, *or the janitor has* to lock the door." "The teacher, the janitor, *or the students have* to lock the door." With a compound subject joined by *or, nor,* or *but,* the verb agrees with the nearest member of the subject.

c) GRAMMAR

"He is the man *who* I think drove the car." (who drove)

"He is the *man* whom I think I saw in the car." (I saw whom)

Watch your comparisons. "The heat stability of silicone rubber is *better than that* (or *than the heat stability*) of organic rubber. Not *"better than organic rubber."*

"Our catcher is *as good as, if not better than,* theirs." Not *as good, if not better than.*

Use parallel grammatical constructions for a series of three or more. "They ate meat *for breakfast, lunch, and dinner."* Not *"for* breakfast, lunch, and *for* dinner."

"The University of California plans *to more than double* classrooms by 1975." Splitting an infinitive may give the shade of meaning you desire. If it does not, why split it?

Beginning sentences with *but, and,* or *or* often makes comprehension easier. *But* makes the heavy parenthetical *however* unnecessary.

Whenever you end a sentence with a preposition naturally, it is acceptable. "He repeated the pledge we had agreed to."

d) PUNCTUATION

Do not use quotation marks for an acceptable colloquialism. "He is a trouble-shooter in our organization." Not "trouble-shooter."

Commas are required on both ends of an appositive. "Stephen Jastrow, our distinguished chairman, will now speak."

It is American practice to place the *period* and the *comma always inside* of the quotation marks; the *colon* and *semicolon always outside* of the quotation marks; the *dash,* the *question mark,* and the *exclamation point inside* of the quotation marks when they apply to the quoted matter only, and *outside* when they apply to the whole sentence.

e) SPELLING

Hyphens are not subject to dependable rules. Use your dictionary or other authority to decide when two nouns are written as two words, hyphenated, or written as one word. Hyphenate compound adjectives before a noun but not after: *pressure-sensitive* tape, but "This tape is *pressure sensitive.*"

"*It's* time you changed *its* oil." The contraction of verbs requires an apostrophe; possessive pronouns do not.

You Should Have Command of Your Language

The somewhat old-fashioned phrase "command of language" indicates a condition rarely reached in presentations today. It is a condition that you should aspire to achieve, in both your oral and written presentations. The effort is not arduous; the rewards, substantial.

Vocabulary. To have a command of your native language implies, first, that your vocabulary has breadth and exactness. It suggests that you choose your words with some sense of their special fitness or eloquence. In making a presentation the average businessman does worse than show a limited vocabulary. He seems to prefer tasteless jargon to plain English. Apart from his addiction to words like *budgetwise, finalize,* and *optimal,* he seems to believe that *prior to* is better than *before, due to the fact that* better than *because,* and *as far as costs are concerned* better than simple *costs.* He seems to prefer *infer* rather than *imply, myself* rather than *me, providing* rather than *provided,* and *disinterested* rather than *uninterested* without being curious about the grounds for his choice.

Pronunciation. If you are to have command of your language, your pronunciation should be accurate and your enunciation clear.

Do not fall into slurrings such as *gover'ment, Sad'dy, mater'al,* and *deter'oration.* Note that the first syllable of *occur, official, efficient,* and *essential* includes both a short vowel and a consonant. Do not affect the mispronunciations oh-cur, oh-ficial, ee-ficient, and ee-sential. If the French *liaison* is a word that you cannot do without, you should know that it has three syllables—*li-ai-son*—and that the first syllable is pronounced [lee] and cannot be pronounced [lay] in any language and never [lie] in French.

Usage. If you are any American besides an English teacher, you probably have split attitudes toward English usage. On the one hand, since technically you know almost nothing about the language you use, you tend to treat the matter lightly. Until you get up to make a presentation, that is. Then unconsciously you are so worried that you may make errors that your speech grows stuttery. But worry does not help. You make gross errors anyhow. Not worrying does not help either. In spite of their own limitations, the members of the average audience are severe in their disapproval when they catch a speaker making grammatical mistakes.

In ordinary spoken English you can make only a handful of errors serious enough to be called gross—and to be noticed by an average audience. What are universally considered gross errors, are violations of the most elementary conventions of speech, just as cleaning your teeth at the table in the United States is considered a gross violation of those conventions we call manners. Anyone who has finished the eighth grade has been taught all he needs to know to avoid substandard usage. Since college graduates habitually make gross errors in their speech, you had better make sure that your oral presentations are not disfigured by such illiteracy.

The gross errors of usage in the speech of otherwise educated persons fill a short list:

a) *Number*

"*There are* [not *is*] several *causes* of crime in this city."
"*This kind* of crime involves violence." "*These kinds* of crimes involve violence." Not *these kind* of crimes.

"A *survey* of the causes of crimes in ten cities *is* [not *are*] being published."

"Crime is a *phenomenon* [not *phenomena*] of our times."

"Even if the police catch a criminal, the court will often let *him* [not *them*] off."

"A prison *term doesn't* [not *don't*] seem to help a young offender."

b) *Case of pronouns* with verbs and prepositions

"The trooper *questioned* my brother and *me* [not *I* or *myself*]."

"*We* [not *us*] *campers called* the trooper, but he wouldn't *believe us* [not *we*] youngsters."

c) *Confusion* of *lie* and *lay, leave* and *let,* and *sit* and *set*

"She *lay* [not *laid*] down for a nap." "She was *lying* [not *laying*] down for a nap." (*lie, lay, lying, have lain*) (*lay, laid, laying, have laid*)

"*Let* [not *leave*] the children go first."

"She *sat* [not *set*] waiting for him." (*sit, sat, sitting, have sat*) (*set, set, setting, have set*)

d) *Real* used in the place of *very*

"The doctor is *very* [not *real*] clever." [Better: is clever.]

"He is pitching *very* [not *real*] well [not *good*]."

When you can say that you never make any of the gross errors just indicated, your presentations will pass one quality control test. But you are not likely to reach even this modest level of literacy without reviewing your elementary school grammar. You cannot possibly choose correct forms consistently by depending on your ear alone. No matter how much you know about eugenics, biophysics, or cash flow, you still are judged by the language you use.

An hour should be enough to bring back such simple matters as transitive and intransitive verbs, prepositions, and nominative and objective case of pronouns, the forms that force choices on you more often than any others. Or if you like, hire a high school teacher as tutor. Her rates will be lower than those of a golf pro.

If you truly aspire to a command of language so that your speech will be correct, fluent, precise, and eloquent, then you must also extend your familiarity with the best English through wide reading of serious books.

Books

Recommended

For Constant Reference

Webster's New Collegiate Dictionary (Merriam) (or similar one)
Any handbook of English for college freshmen
Appropriate professional society instructions

For Careful Reading

Technical Report Writing, Fred H. Rhodes
The Presentation of Technical Information, Reginald O. Kapp
The Art of Working with People, Edward Hodnett
Technical Reporting, Joseph N. Ulman, Jr.
The Language of Science, William Gilman
How to Write Scientific and Technical Papers, Sam F. Trelease
The Art of Persuasion, Wayne C. Minnich
When It's Your Turn to Speak, Orvin Larson
How to Talk with People, Irving J. Lee
How to Run More Effective Business Meetings, B. Y. Auger
The Art of Problem Solving, Edward Hodnett

For Consulting

A Dictionary of Contemporary American Usage, Bergen Evans
and Cornelia Evans

A Dictionary of Modern Usage, H. W. Fowler (1965 ed. revised by Sir Ernest Gowers)

Current American Usage, Margaret M. Bryant

The Elements of Style, W. Strunk, Jr. and E. B. White

Presentation of Ideas, NavExos P-1516, U.S. Government Printing Office

Information and Communication Practice in Industry, T. E. R. Singer

Communicating Facts and Ideas in Business, Leland Brown

Readings in Communication from Fortune, Francis W. Weeks (ed.)

Technical and Professional Writing: A Practical Anthology, Herman A. Estrin (ed.)

Elementary Business Statistics, John E. Freund and Frank J. Williams

Thinking Straight, Monroe C. Beardsley

Index